ATLAS of the Pacific Northwest

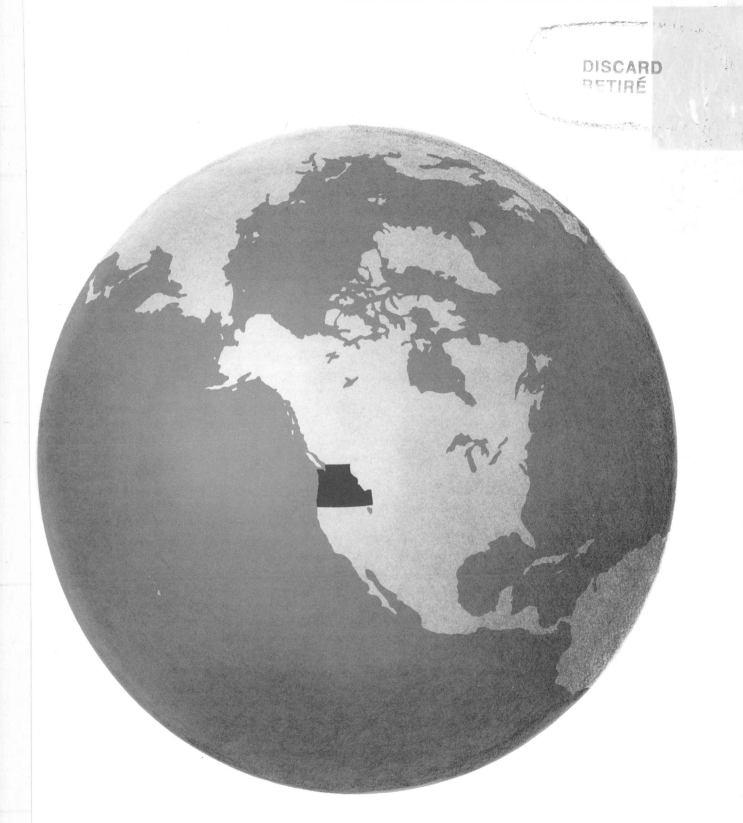

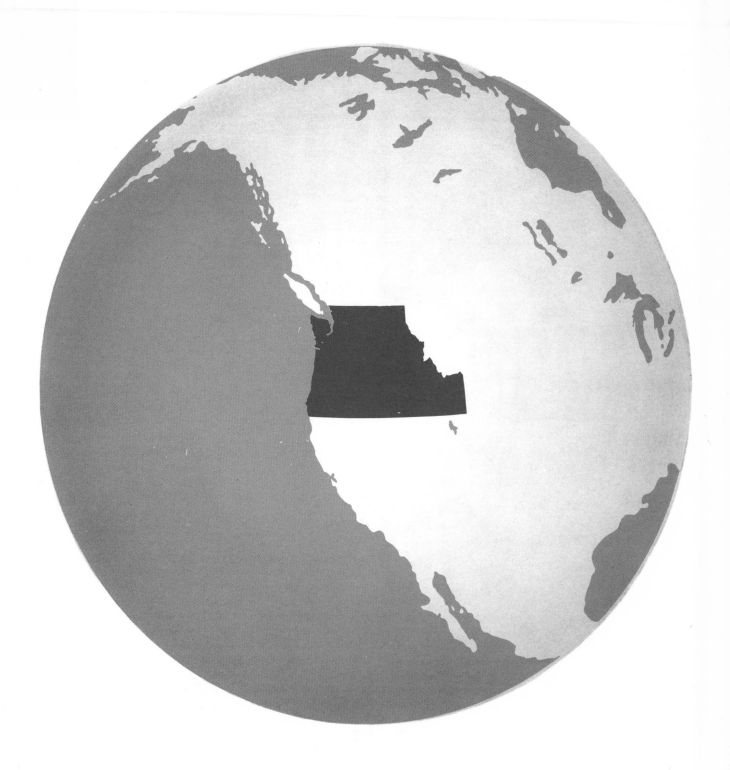

ATLAS of the Pacific Northwest

Richard M. Highsmith Jr., *editor*

Robert Bard, *cartographer*

5th Edition
Oregon State University Press
Corvallis

Acknowledgments

The fifth edition of the *Atlas of the Pacific Northwest* is a complete revision and another stage in the plan of Oregon State University Press to maintain a current and convenient regional source book. In comparison with the fourth edition, the dimensions of this volume have been slightly reduced to improve shelving; the text has been markedly decreased and the graphic materials increased to portray more readily the spatial character of the Pacific Northwest. The variety of topic coverage has been expanded, and the region has been redefined to exclude western Montana to increase the availability and uniformity of data. These changes represent a consensus of user opinions of ways to augment the utility of the *Atlas*.

Except for J. Kenneth Munford, Director of Oregon State University Press, the contributors to this edition are members of the faculty of the Department of Geography, Oregon State University. Their contributions are indicated within the volume.

Those who deserve special recognition for the help they gave the editor and authors in compiling basic data and photographs and in drafting graphics include Anne Adams, Richard Beck, John Beckley, Jack Blok, Edward Bovy, Wayne Britton, Jack Burk, David Buset, Bryan Christian, Sandra Dunn, Richard East, Susan Edwards, David Fenton, Dennis Frates, Roland Grant, Judith Hedberg, Herschel Henderly, Joseph Herzig, Robin Keleher, Brent Lake, Rosemary McLeod, Dennis Oaks, Arthur Rathburn, Joseph Szramek, Stephen Snyder, Charles Stevens, John Stockham, Roberta Stream, Timothy Tolle, Harry Utti, and Larry Vinton.

RICHARD M. HIGHSMITH, JR.

Third Edition © 1962
Fourth Edition © 1968
Fifth Edition © 1973
OREGON STATE UNIVERSITY PRESS
Corvallis, Oregon 97330

Library of Congress card catalog number: Map 62-50

ISBN: O-87071-406-6 (paper); 0-87071-407-4 (cloth)

Printed in the United States of America

Photo Credits

Abbreviations used for contributors:

IDCD	Idaho Department of Commerce and Development, Boise
OHS	Oregon Historical Society, Portland
OSHD	Oregon State Highway Department, Salem
USBIA	U. S. Bureau of Indian Affairs
USBR	U. S. Bureau of Reclamation
USCE	U. S. Corps of Engineers
USFS	U. S. Forest Service
USNPS	U. S. National Park Service
USSCS	U. S. Soil Conservation Service
WSDC	Washington State Department of Commerce, Olympia

Page 3: Gem, Idaho, *R. W. Smith;* Seattle, *Seattle-First National Bank;* Northern Pacific special, *OHS;* Wasco warehouse, *OHS;* early motorists, *OHS;* Banks, Oregon, *C. W. Munford.*

Pages 4, 6: historical maps, *OHS.*

Pages 7,8,10,11: historical maps, *Oregon State Library.*

Pages 16-17: *National Aeronautics and Space Administration-ERTS-1.*

Page 33: Cape Falcon, *OSHD;* Okanogan mountains, *USFS;* Cle Elum storage dam, *USBR;* Central Oregon, *USBIA;* Hells Canyon, *IDCD.*

Pages 35-38: Coast Range, *OSHD;* Willamette Valley, *OSHD;* North Cascades, *USNPS;* Central Cascades, *OSHD;* Palouse hills, *John S. Shelton;* Snake River plain, *John S. Shelton, GEOLOGY ILLUSTRATED,* © *W. H. Freeman and Co.;* Abert Rim, *John S. Shelton;* Smoky Mountains, *John S. Shelton.*

Page 55: Upper slope vegetation, *David Simons;* all others, *USFS.*

Page 59: (drawing) *Oregon State University Press.*

Pages 64-65: Harvest pattern, *OSHD;* log truck, *Western Wood Products Association;* cattle on range, *USSCS;* stream in forest, *OSHD;* dam, *WSDC;* irrigation, *USSCS.*

Page 66: Grand Coulee Dam, *USBR.*

Page 87: both pictures, *USBR.*

Page 96: Centralia coal field, *Pacific Power and Light Co.;* gravel operation, *USCE.*

Pages 102-103: Astoria, *OSHD;* Oregon City, *Crown Zellerbach Corp.;* Springfield, *Weyerhaeuser;* Vancouver, *Delano Studios and Aerial Surveys;* Seattle, *Port of Seattle;* copper smelter, *Harry R. Boersig.*

Page 111: *Columbia Shopping Center, Inc.;* Lloyd Center, *Photo Art Commercial Studio.*

Page 112: Willamette River, *Ackroyd Photography, Inc.*

Page 116: (left top to bottom) Paradise Valley and Mount Rainier, *USNPS;* upper north fork of Bridge Creek meadows, northern Cascades, Washington, *David Simons;* beach at Rooster Rock State Park, *OSHD;* (right) Lake Coeur d'Alene, Idaho, *IDCD;* Multnomah Falls, *OSHD.*

ARRANGEMENT OF TOPICS AND GRAPHICS

A picture is said to be worth a thousand words. On that basis a map may be said to be worth a thousand pictures.

—L. A. HEINDL, 1971

SOURCES OF DATA

Computer maps, endpaper
Authority: David L. Buset
Sources: Plots produced by SURGE 2. Programs written by Marks S. Monmonier with extensive modifications by Frank T. Aldrich. Compilation of Willamette Valley and Puget Sound plots by David L. Buset.

Two Centuries of Development pp. 3-15
Authority: J. Kenneth Munford
Sources: (**maps**) Details from (page 4) A New Map of the Whole Continent, North America, by Robt. Sayer, London, 1786; A New Map of North America from the Latest Authorities, John Cary, engr., London, 1806; A Map of North America by Samuel Walker, Boston, ca. 1825; (page 6) Map of Oregon Territory by the U.S. Exploring Expedition, Charles Wilkes, Esqr., Commander, 1841; (page 7) Map of U.S. Territory of Oregon, M. H. Stansbury, del., Washington, D.C., 1838; (page 8) A New Map of Texas, Oregon, and California [used by immigrants and gold seekers over Oregon and California trails] pub. by S. A. Mitchell, Philadelphia, 1846. (page 9) Willamette Meridian adapted from A Diagram of a Portion of the Oregon Territory, U.S. Surveyor General, 1851; (page 11) Colton's Washington and Oregon, New York, 1859; (page 12) Map of Oregon, Washington, Idaho, and part of Montana, pub. by S. A. Mitchell, Philadelphia, 1877.
(**text**) Dorothy O. Johansen and C. M. Gates, Empire of the Columbia, 1957; G. W. Fuller, History of the Pacific Northwest, 1931; Charles H. Carey, History of Oregon, 1922; Federal Writers' Project: The Idaho Encyclopedia, 1938, Idaho, A Guide in Word and Picture, 1950, Oregon, The End of the Trail, 1940, Washington, A Guide to the Evergreen State, 1941; R. B. Whitebrook, Coastal Exploration of Washington, 1959; H. R. Wagner, Spanish Explorations in the Strait of Juan de Fuca, 1971; F. W. Howay, Voyages of the Columbia, 1941; Oregon Blue Book, "Chronology of the Oregon Country" 1973; H. M. Corning, Dictionary of Oregon History, 1956; Henry Villard, Early History of Transportation in Oregon, 1944. For place names references see page 13.
(**consultants**) Merle W. Wells, Idaho State Historical Society; Kenneth L. Holmes, Oregon College of Education; William G. Robbins, Oregon State University; staff, Oregon Historical Society.

Population, Urbanization, Labor Force pp. 18-25.
Authority: Ray M. Northam
Sources: U. S. Bureau of the Census. U. S. Census of Population: 1970.

Transportation and Circulation pp. 26-32
Authority: Ray M. Northam
Sources: National Atlas; Pacific Northwest River Basins Commission, Columbia-North Pacific Region Comprehensive Framework Study of Water and Related Lands, Appendix II, Appendix X; Richard Preston, Economic Geography, 1970; Federal Power Commission, Typical Electric Bills, 1972.

Landforms pp. 34-43
Authority: Robert Bard
Sources: Bates McKee, Cascadia, The Geologic Evolution of the Pacific Northwest, 1972; William D. Thornburg, Regional Geomorphology of the United States, 1965; Samuel H. Dicken, Oregon Geography, 1965; Ira S. Allison, Physical Provinces, map of Northwestern States, 1968; Edwin H. Hammond, Classes of Land-Surface Form in the 48 states, map, 1964; Geology, National Atlas Map, 1966.

Climates pp. 43-54
Authority: James F. Lahey
Sources: Climatic Atlas of the United States, U. S. Dept. of Commerce, Environmental Science Services Administration, June 1968; Climate and Man, Yearbook of Agriculture, 1941, U. S. Dept. of Agriculture, 1942; Harold Crutcher. Upper Wind Statistics Charts of the Northern Hemisphere, Vol. I-Navaer 50-IC-535, U. S. Navy, August 1959; U. S. Dept. of the Interior, Geological Survey, The National Atlas of the United States of America, Washington, D. C., 1970, Climate Section pp. 93-116; C. R. Hosler, Low Level Inversion Frequency in the Contiguous United States, Monthly Weather Review, 89(9); Sept. 1961; Climatological Handbook, Vol. II—Precipitation, Columbia Basin States, Meteorological Committee, Pacific N. W. River Basins Commission, Sept. 1969; Val Leonard Mitchell, The Regionalization of Climate in Montana Areas, Ph.D. thesis, University of Wisconsin, Madison, 1969.

Vegetation pp. 55-58
Authority: Robert E. Frenkel
Sources: A Cronquist, *et al.* Intermountain Flora, Vol. I, 1972; R. Daubenmire, Steppe Vegetation of Washington, Wash. Agri. Exp. Sta. Tech. Bull. 62, 1970); R. Daubenmire and J. B. Daubenmire, Forest Vegetation of Eastern Washington and Northern Idaho, Wash. Agri. Ext. Sta. Tech. Bull. 60, 1968; J. F. Franklin and C. T. Dyrness, Vegetation of Oregon and Washington, Pacific Northwest For. and Range Exp. Sta. Res. Pap. PNW-80, 1969; A. W. Küchler, Potential Natural Vegetation of the Conterminous United States, Amer. Geog. Soc. Publ., No. 36, 1964; E. L. Little, Jr., Atlas of United States, Trees, Vol. 1, Conifers and Important Hardwoods, USDA Miscell. Publ. No. 1146, 1971.

Soils pp. 59-63
Authority: Robert F. Frenkel
Sources: Distribution of Principal Kinds of Soils, Orders, Suborders, and Great Groups, National Atlas Map, 1967; Soil Classification, A Comprehensive System, Soil Conservation Service, 1960; Land Capability Maps, Oregon, Washington, Idaho, Soil Conservation Service.

Water pp. 67-75
Authority: Keith W. Muckleston
Sources: USGS Water Supply Paper 1797. Pacific Northwest River Basins Commission Columbia-North Pacific Region. Comprehensive Framework Study, Appendices V Vol. 1 and 2, VII, X, XI, XII; Power Planning Committee, PNWRBC, Review of Power Planning in the Pacific Northwest; Water Resources Council, The Nation's Water Resources; Corps of Engineers, North Pacific Division, Recreation Use Data; Bureau of Reclamation Region I, Recreation Use Data; Soil Conservation Service, Maps of PL-566 Projects.

Agriculture pp. 76-86
Authority: Richard M. Highsmith, Jr.
Sources: Bureau of Reclamation, Region I irrigation maps; Soil Conservation Service, land capability maps; Pacific Northwest River Basins Commission, Columbia-North Pacific

Region Comprehensive Framework Study of Water and Related Lands (1970-71); 1969 Census of Agriculture.

Forest Resources and Industries pp 88-93
Authority: J. Granville Jensen
Sources: Pacific Northwest Range and Experiment Station, U. S. Forest Service, Resource Bulletin PNW 9, Timber Resources Statistics For The Pacific Northwest, 1965; Brian R. Wall, Projected Development of the Timber Economy of the Columbia-North Pacific Region, 1969, U. S. Forest Service Resource Bulletin PNW-38, Oregon Timber Harvest, 1971; U. S. Forest Service Resource Bulletin PNW-37, Washington Timber Harvest, 1971; U. S. Forest Service, Research Notes INT-132, Estimates of Timber Products Output and Plant Residue, Idaho, 1971; Lockwood's Directory of the Pulp and Paper Industry, 1971-72; Directory of Forest Products Industry, 1971.

Fisheries Resources pp. 94-95
Authority: J. Granville Jensen
Sources: Fish Commission of Oregon, Commercial Food Fish Landings in Pounds Round Weight by State of Oregon Administrative Districts for Calendar Year 1970, 1971; Washington Department of Fisheries, 1970 Fisheries Statistical Report, 1971; Fisheries Statistics of the United States 1960-1971.

Mineral Resources pp. 97-101
Authority: Thomas J. Maresh
Sources: Walter E. Lewis, Liaison Officer, U. S. Bureau of Mines, Salem, Oregon; U. S. Bureau of Mines, Minerals Yearbook (various years).

Manufacturing pp. 104-110
Authority: Thomas J. Maresh
Sources: U. S. Bureau of the Census, Census of Manufacturers, 1967; State of Washington, Department of Commerce and Economic Development, Manufacturers' Guide, 1969; Idaho Department of Commerce and Development, Manufacturing Directory of Idaho; State of Oregon, Economic Development Division, Directory of Oregon Manufacturers, 1968 and 1972. U. S. Bureau of Census, County and City Data Book.

Trade and Service Activity pp. 113-115
Authority: Ray M. Northam
Sources: U. S. Bureau of the Census, U. S. Census of Population 1970; General Social and Economic Characteristics.

Recreation pp. 117-127
Authority: Oliver H. Heintzelman
Sources: Oregon State Highway Commission; Wash. State Parks and Recreation Commission; Idaho State Dept. of Commerce and Development; Wash. State Department of Commerce and Economic Development; USDA-Forest Service-National Forest Maps; USDI-Bureau of Land Management, Fish and Wildlife Service, Bureau of Sports Fisheries and Wildlife, and National Park Service; Bowmer, J. L. and Meyer, N. G. (Published by J. R. Rogers), *The Rockhound's Map of Wash.*; J. R. Rogers, Idaho and Oregon Rock Deposits.

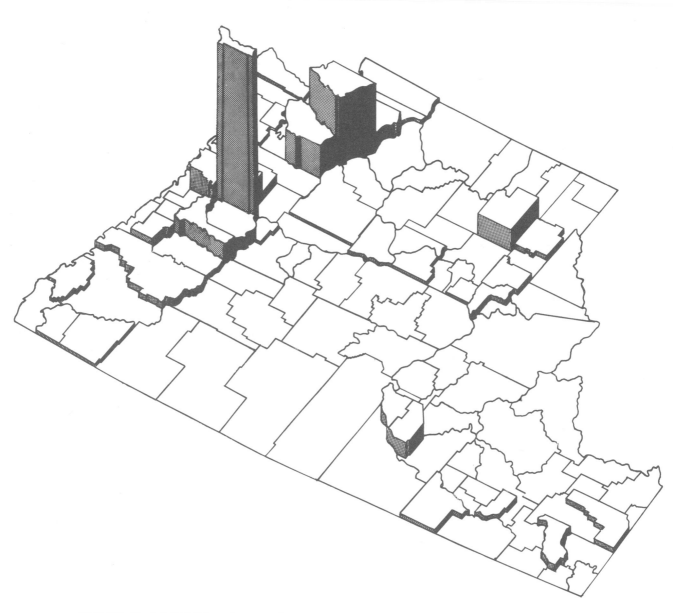

POPULATION of each county in the Pacific Northwest
with height proportional to density per square mile, and
volume proportional to population.

Washington
  Land area _____ 66,663 square miles
  Water area _____ 1,529 square miles
  General coastline _____ 157 statute miles
  Tidal shoreline _____ 3,026 statute miles

Oregon
  Land area _____ 96,209 square miles
  Water area _____ 772 square miles
  General coastline _____ 296 statute miles
  Tidal shoreline _____ 1,410 statute miles

Idaho
  Land area _____ 82,677 square miles
  Water area _____ 880 square miles

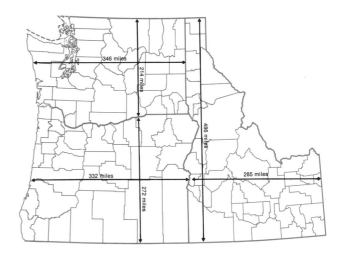

1

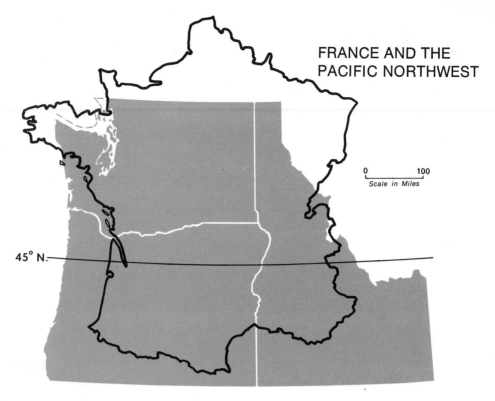

FRANCE AND THE
PACIFIC NORTHWEST

0   100
Scale in Miles

45° N.

KEY TO COUNTIES

HISTORICAL GLIMPSES of the Pacific Northwest

(above) Mining town in a Coeur d'Alene canyon. Gem, Idaho, 1902

Seattle in 1866. Hilltop building with white columns is the University of the Territory of Washington.

(right, top down) Northern Pacific Railroad special for gold-spike ceremony; first through train from Great Lakes to Portland, September 1883

Sheep pelt warehouse and ten-horse team at Wasco, Oregon, at turn of the century

Early motorists at Madras, Oregon, 1910

Typical small town west of the Cascades, Banks, Oregon, 1909

WHITE MEN first set foot intentionally on what is now the Pacific Northwest—the states of Oregon, Washington, and Idaho—only two hundred years ago. Wrecked ships with men aboard may have washed ashore before then, but the record is not clear.

The discoveries made and changes wrought by the invaders in these two centuries have found expression in the changing, ever-more detailed maps of the region. Just as the land is formed by strata laid down in successive geological ages, names on the land reflect successive layers of exploration, settlement, and development.

The native inhabitants, who have lived here for at least 9,000 years—perhaps twice that long—had names for many geographical features. The newcomers—explorers, hunters, traders, missionaries, settlers, surveyors, legislators, road and railroad builders, and real estate developers—sometimes continued use of Indian names, but more often bestowed new ones.

Having no written language and an oral language the visitors could not translate precisely, the natives used signs and crude maps drawn on the ground to communicate geographical information. The visitors wrote what they heard in a variety of ways.

The name of a tribe on the Oregon coast, for example, appeared on maps or in print as *Kilamuke, Kilamox, Killimoux, Killamouck, Callemeux,* and *Cal-a-mex* before before becoming TILLAMOOK.

Ee-dah-how!, a Shoshoni exclamation announcing the sun coming down the mountain, heralding a new day, became IDAHO.

The promoters who platted the town that has become the metropolis of the Pacific Northwest wanted to name an area the Indians called *Mulckmukum, Duwamps,* and *Tzee-tzee-lal-itch* for a friendly chief of the Duwamish and Suquamish tribes. He was known as *See-alt, See-ualt, See-yat, Sealth,* and *Se-at-tlh.* The developers decided to call it SEATTLE.

Other cities in the region have names adapted from Indian words: Tacoma, "snowy mountain"; Wenatchee, "river flowing from canyon"; Walla Walla, "running water"; and Spokane, Yakima, Klamath Falls, and Pocatello for tribes or chiefs.

Of the 119 counties in the three states, 15 in Washington, 9 in Oregon, and 7 in Idaho have Indian names such as Klickitat, Snohomish, Skagit, Multnomah, Clackamas, Wallowa, Kootenai, Bannock, and Minidoka. (See tables, page 13.)

Many other geographical features still bear Indian names, but for the most part, the newcomers—not knowing, nor caring to learn, or not able to determine Indian names—put names they already knew and could recognize on their maps and in their reports to identify places they wanted to remember. They used descriptive words or phrases—Blanco, Foulweather, Flattery, Destruction, Shoalwater, Lookout, Clearwater, Boise, Twin Falls. They commemorated saints—San Juan, Perpetua, Rosalia, Sebastian, St. Paul, St. Maries.

They rewarded members of crews and exploring parties—Baker, Puget, Whidbey, John Day, Owyhee. They recognized sponsors and leaders of expeditions—the Admiralty, Lord Hood, Vancouver, Gray, Lewis, Clark, Astor, McKenzie, Whitman, Stevens, Mullan. They remembered places back home, friends, national and classical figures, wives and daughters, and invented new names.

The experienced woodsmen from French Canada, whom the U.S., Canadian, and English fur traders brought in as employees or partners, left French names such as Coeur d'Alene, Nez Percé, Pend Orielle, Payette, La Biche, Deschutes, Grande Ronde, and La Grande.

Spaniards from New Spain (Mexico) came first. They sailed along the California and Oregon coasts in the 16th and 17th centuries. Beginning in 1571 they carried on transpacific trade with their colony in the Philippines for 200 years. The most direct route, following the Great Circle, between Mexico and Manila lay along the west coast, the Aleutians, and Japan. Prevailing westerly winds favored a northerly route on the return trip and there is evidence of a Spanish galleon having been wrecked on the Oregon coast. Official records indicate that sea-going Spanish exploring parties reached 42° north latitude as early as 1542 and farther north in 1603. Capes Ferrelo, (San) Sebastian, and Blanco and Heceta Head are reminders on the Oregon coast of early Spanish explorers.

The Spaniards did not give wide publicity to their activities or discoveries until years later. The English also kept their first voyage to the Pacific, that of Francis Drake in 1578-79, secret for a while, but eventually announced that he had landed on the west coast and had taken possession of what he called New Albion for Queen Elizabeth. British mapmakers called the coast north of California New Albion for more than 200 years. (See the 1838 map, next page.)

The published charts of later English explorations, most notably those of Cook (1778) and Vancouver (1792), helped acquaint the world with this new territory. When English cartographers had sufficient information, they included Indian and Spanish names, but more often used those brought home by their own expeditions, superseding previous ones.

Naming the peak on the peninsula in northwest Washington serves as an example. At the time of the first recorded sighting of the Washington coast, in June 1774, Juan Perez named the peak *El Cerro de la Santa Rosalia*, but his chart was not published for many years. When a flamboyant former English naval lieutenant, John Meares, sighted the same mountain 14 years later he called it Mount Olympus and let other explorers know where to look for the Olympics.

A year after Perez sighted the Washington coast, Bruno Heceta and Bodega y Quadra made the first landings. In July 1775, Heceta went ashore at a point a little south of Mt. Olympus, erected a cross, and took possession of the land for Spain. Seven crewmen Quadra sent ashore at the mouth of the Moclips River the same day were ambushed and killed by Indians. The point was called *Punta de los Martires* and an island farther north *Delores* in memory of the martyrs. Twelve years later a boatload of men from Captain Barkley's ship also met a tragic fate in this vicinity. Destruction Island commemorates these massacres.

By a curious combination of legend and events, the broad strait north of the Olympic peninsula retained a Spanish name. In 1592, according to an unreliable account published in England 30 years later, a Greek sailor, Apostolos Valerianos, using the name Juan de Fuca accompanied a Spanish ship along the northwest coast. He told of discovering a passageway into an inland sea. Mapmakers thereafter began to show the Strait of Juan de Fuca at 48°-49° north latitude as the opening into the River of the West.

In 1787, nearly 200 years after de Fuca's supposed discovery, an English sea captain, Charles Barkley, sailing under an Austrian flag, came to Vancouver Island, accompanied by his young wife, the first white woman to visit this coast. In her diary she wrote, "To our great astonishment, we arrived off a large opening extending eastward . . . which my husband immediately recognized as the long lost strait of Juan de Fuca, and to which he gave the name of the original discoverer." The next year, John Meares, sailing under a Portuguese flag, also came upon the strait, acknowledged the legendary Greek, and in publicizing his feats perpetuated the name of Juan de Fuca.

Earlier, when Captain James Cook came in 1778, he named Capes Foulweather, Perpetua, and Gregory (Arago) in Oregon, missed finding the Strait of Juan de Fuca, but named Cape Flattery in Washington. He landed in Nootka Sound on Vancouver Island and there found an abundance of furs, which his crewmen purchased for bedding and clothing.

When news that these crewmen a year later had sold their worn and dirty furs in China at immense profit reached Europe and eastern America, traders from many nations under many flags flocked to the northwest coast. Spain, France, and England sent exploring expeditions.

In 1790 and 1791, Spanish parties under Quimper and Eliza charted the Juan de Fuca strait. Subsequent English and American surveyors replaced nearly all of the Spanish names, but a few reminders of this period remain: Cape Alava, Port Angeles (*Puerto Nuestra Señora de los Angeles*); Haro and Rosario straits; San Juan, Patos, Sucia, Matia, Guemes, and Orcas islands; and Padilla Bay.

On a Sunday morning in April 1792, ships of a Yankee fur trader and a British sea captain met by chance near Destruction Island. Robert Gray of Boston was looking for safe anchorages where he could trade with friendly natives. George Vancouver, who had been a midshipman with Cook 14 years before, had come to chart the coast and negotiate with the Spaniards. Gray and Vancouver exchanged information that April morning, then went their separate ways.

Gray had heard Spanish reports of a Great River of the West and earlier had sighted what he thought was its mouth. Cruising south along the coast he entered a harbor —subsequently known as Bulfinch's, Whidbey's and now Gray's—where he traded and had a skirmish with the Indians.

A few days later he located the mouth of a large river farther south and succeeded in taking his ship, the *Columbia Rediviva*, across the bar. He named the river Columbia for his ship and the point south of the entrance for President John Adams. Meares had already named the point north of the entrance Cape Disappointment, because he

1841

MAPS like this sample and reports of Lt. Charles Wilkes' 1841 expedition to the Oregon Country gave the U.S. information about rivers and harbors, settlements, and natural resources.

The native Americans had crisscrossed and traded extensively through the region for a long time to supply their own needs. Now the white men began to probe into the interior to examine resources and investigate commercial opportunities. To inquire about possibilities of expanding the fur trade overland from the east, Alexander McKenzie of the North West Company of Montreal crossed Canada to the Pacific in 1793, adding his store of knowledge to that of earlier explorers.

In the 19th century, as the following chronology indicates, the map of the Pacific Northwest began to fill up at an ever-increasing pace.

19th Century Chronology

1804-06 Meriwether Lewis and William Clark, sent by President Jefferson to explore northern part of new Louisiana Purchase and the Columbia Basin, cross Rocky Mountains, descend the Clearwater, Snake, and Columbia rivers, build Fort Clatsop for winter quarters near mouth of Columbia, and return to U.S. with many sketch maps and much information.

1807-11 David Thompson, North West Company geographer and trader, explores western Canada, builds posts on Pend Oreille Lake and near Spokane, and descends Columbia to the mouth.

1810 Efforts of Winship brothers of Boston to establish a post and farm on lower Columbia thwarted by spring floods.

1811 John Jacob Astor, New York merchant, sends two parties, one by sea, one overland, to found Astoria as a permanent post at mouth of Columbia.

1812 Astor partner, Wilson Price Hunt and party (including John Day for whom rivers, etc., are named) arrives at Astoria after arduous overland journey. Donald McKenzie and other Astorians explore "the Garden of the Columbia" (Willamette Valley), find plentiful game and the McKenzie River.

Astorian Robert Stuart and party, returning east, blaze a shorter route that later becomes the Oregon Trail.

1813 Astor partners at Astoria, fearful that a British warship will take their post by force, sell it to the North West Company of Montreal.

1814-15 Treaty of Ghent after War of 1812 returns Astoria to U.S., but Astor no longer interested in maintaining it.

1818 Joint occupancy of the Oregon Country for 10 years agreed to by U.S. and Great Britain; Canadians continue to dominate fur trade of the region.

1821-27 North West and Hudson's Bay companies combine under name of the latter (HBC) in 1821. Dr. John McLoughlin appointed chief factor (1824), moves headquarters to Fort Vancouver (1825), and becomes virtual ruler of region for two decades. Farms and small manufacturing started at Fort Vancouver, sawmill in 1827.

1827 Agreement on joint occupancy extended by U.S. and G.B. for 10 years.

1828 Jedediah Smith, American frontiersman, by way of northern California and western Oregon, arrives at Ft. Vancouver.

HBC builds grist mills at Fort Vancouver and Fort Colville.

1828-33 Independent farming begins in Willamette Valley when Etienne Lucier and other French-Canadians who had helped found Astoria and were later employed by HBC settle on French Prairie north of Salem.

1829 Other former HBC employees settle at Willamette Falls (Oregon City), starting town that later becomes first incorporated city and capital of the territory.

Mountain Man Joe Meek struggles with HBC for fur trade in Snake River country, later becomes prominent settler in Tualatin Valley west of Portland.

1831 Frontiersman Kit Carson winters on Salmon River in Idaho.

had failed to recognize the mouth of the river when he passed it.

On the coast Vancouver renamed "Point of the Martyrs" Point Grenville and then turned into the Strait of Juan de Fuca. Filling in his charts he named Admiralty Inlet, Hood's Canal, Mt. Rainier, Bellingham Bay, and Vashon Island for Navy colleagues; (New) Dungeness for his home port in England; Mt. Baker, Port Orchard, Whidbey Island, and Puget Sound for diligent crew members; Protection Island, Port Discovery, Deception Pass, and other locations. On the birthday of King George III he landed at Possession Sound (Everett), called the new land he was exploring New Georgia, and took possession of it in the name of the king.

Gray and Vancouver met at Nootka Sound later in the summer of 1792 and exchanged information again. Vancouver then sent Lt. Broughton south to investigate the newly discovered river. Broughton rowed up the Columbia as far as the Sandy River, naming Tongue Point, Young's Bay, Puget and Walker islands, Coffin Mountain, Mt. St. Helens, and Mt. Hood. He honored Gray as first to enter the river with Gray's Bay and Gray's River. Published in 1798, Vancouver's charts tended to fix permanent names on many Pacific Northwest places, although what he called Cape Orford (on some maps Oxford) on the Oregon coast has retained its older Spanish name, Cape Blanco.

1838

MAP
of the
UNITED STATES
TERRITORY OF OREGON
West of the Rocky Mountains

Exhibiting the various Trading Depots or Forts
occupied by the British Hudson Bay Company connected with the Western and northwestern Fur Trade.

Compiled in the Bureau of Topographical
Engineers from the latest authorities under
the direction of Col. J.J. Abert by
Wash: Hood.
1838.
M.H.Stansbury del.

The prolongation of the 49ᵗʰ parallel of latitude from the Rocky
Mountains to the Pacific has been assumed as the Northern Boundary
of the U.States possessions on the N.W. coast, in consequence of
the following extract from the Hon. H.Clays letter to M.ʳ Gallatin
dated June 19ᵗʰ 1826. (see Doc.199. 20ᵗʰ Cong.1.sess.Ho. of R.) You are
then authorized to propose the annulment of the third article of the
Convention of 1818, and the extension of the line on the parallel of
49 from the eastern side of the Stony Mountains, where it now
terminates, to the Pacific Ocean as the permanent boundary
between the territories of the two powers in that quarter. This is
our ultimatum and so you may announce it.

The Posts of the British Hudsons Bay Company are marked thus. ○

PACIFIC OCEAN

NEW CALEDONIA

BRITISH TERRITORY

SASKATCHAWAN

BLOOD

BLACKFOOT

TERRITORY

OF

OREGON

CALIFORNIA

MEXICO

NEW GEORGIA

NEW CORNWALL

NEW ALBION

Northern Boundary 1818

Southern Boundary 1819

SCALES.

Longitude West from Greenwich

1832 Nathaniel J. Wyeth of Boston comes to Vancouver to attempt commercial ventures such as curing and packing salmon and raising tobacco to sell to the Indians; he fails and returns east.

John Ball, Dartmouth College graduate who came with Wyeth, employed by McLoughlin to teach school at Fort Vancouver.

HBC builds Fort Umpqua.

1832-35 Captain B. L. E. de Bonneville, U.S. Army officer on leave, explores and attempts fur trading in Idaho; McLoughlin refuses to sell him trading goods.

1833 HBC builds Fort Nisqually trading post and farm on Puget Sound (near present site of Dupont).

1834 HBC builds Fort Boise on Snake River.

Ewing Young, American trapper, and Hall J. Kelley, Oregon promoter, bring herd of horses overland from California; treated as horse thieves.

On second trip west, Wyeth builds Fort Hall (near Pocatello) and Fort William on Sauvie's Island; latter fails.

Rev. Jason Lee, member of Wyeth party, preaches first sermon in region at Ft. Hall, later founds Methodist mission on French Prairie in Willamette Valley.

Thomas Nuttall, naturalist, surveys plant and bird life.

David Douglas, botanist, after ten years of study has classified hundreds of plants; dies in the Sandwich Islands.

1835 HBC builds sawmill to export lumber from Fort Vancouver.

1836 Dr. Marcus Whitman, Rev. Henry H. Spalding, their wives (first white women to come to Oregon overland), and oth-

ers establish missions and farms, the Whitmans at Waiilatpu (near Walla Walla) and the Spaldings at Lapwai (near Lewiston). Spalding sets up first printing press in region (1839).

HBC buys Fort Hall from Wyeth.

1837 Ewing Young drives herd of cattle from California, becomes prosperous farmer near Newberg, Oregon.

American missionary reinforcements arrive by sea.

First independent farmer settles on Cowlitz Prairie, near Toledo, Washington.

1838 HBC forms subsidiary company to farm on Cowlitz Prairie.

Catholic Fathers Blanchet and Demers, in response to petitions of French-Canadian settlers and HBC employees, arrive at Fort Vancouver via Colville, Okanagan, and Walla Walla.

1839 Catholic mission started at St. Paul on French Prairie with branches at Cowlitz and Nisqually.

Peoria Party of settlers arrives from Illinois.

1840 First permanent settler in Idaho, Wm. Craig, starts farm near Lapwai.

Father De Smet, later active in missions throughout region, conducts services at Pierre's Hole (Teton County), Idaho.

1841 Death of Ewing Young results in formation of a rudimentary government to probate his large estate.

Great Reinforcement of men and women for Methodist missions arrives by sea.

For HBC, James Sinclair leads party from Red River (Winnipeg) over Canadian Rockies and down the Columbia to provide settlers for Nisqually and Cowlitz company farms.

Lt. Charles Wilkes, USN, surveys and charts lower Columbia and Puget Sound. One of his ships, the *Peacock,* wrecked on Peacock Spit at mouth of Columbia. He sends one exploring party to eastern Washington via Naches Pass to Okanogan, Spokane House, Colville, Lapwai, Waiilatpu, Yakima, and back to Nisqually. Another party goes through western Oregon into California. Wilkes' reports, in which he urges U.S. control of Puget Sound for its fine anchorages, and charts provide best account of the region by an American up to that time.

Star of Oregon built at Swan Island (Portland) by Americans, partially outfitted by Wilkes, sails to San Francisco, is sold, and proceeds used to buy cattle to be driven back to Oregon.

1842 First Catholic mission in Idaho built on St. Joe River, later moved to Cataldo near Kellogg, where Father Ravalli and Indian laborers build (1848-53) large church, oldest structure still standing in Idaho.

First college in far west, Willamette University, established as Oregon Institute in Salem. (See table for other early colleges.) Catholic boys school established at St. Paul on French Prairie.

Dr. Elijah White arrives with 120 additional U.S. citizens.

Dr. Whitman rides east to get support for missions; arouses interest in Oregon.

McLoughlin designs plan for Oregon City at Willamette Falls.

1843 Oregon Provisional Government forms at Champoeg, HBC trading post on Willamette; Oregon City selected as seat of government.

Large influx of immigrants in Willamette Valley.

J. J. Audubon classifies birds in Rocky Mountains.

Lt. John C. Fremont, USA, charts Columbia above Wilkes survey, explores central Oregon (Winter Ridge, Summer Lake, Lake Abert) and on into California.

1844 Immigrants over Oregon Trail number 1,475.

Catholic sisters open convent school on French Prairie.

1845 Two British Army lieutenants arrive incognito to survey territory in case of war.

George Abernathy installed as first provisional governor of Oregon and amended organic laws approved by voters.

To avoid difficulty of passing the Cascade Rapids in the Columbia Gorge, Samuel K. Barlow blazes trail from The Dalles south of Mt. Hood into the Willamette Valley; later developed as toll road; although most arduous section of Oregon Trail a large proportion of covered wagons use this route.

Michael T. Simmons and party first American settlers on Puget Sound, at Tumwater.

An estimated 6,000 persons have settled in Oregon, principally in Clatsop, Tualatin, Yamhill, Champoeg, and Clackamas counties.

1846 Joint occupancy ends when treaty with Great Britain makes 49° north latitude boundary between U.S. and Canada west of Rocky Mountains; HBC moves headquarters to Victoria; McLoughlin resigns as chief factor, moves to Oregon City to engage in commercial ventures despite much dissension in community, becomes American citizen and a Roman Catholic in 1849, dies in 1857.

Settlement at Olympia begins.

Oregon Spectator begins publication at Oregon City; first mail contract let.

Applegate brothers and other immigrants of 1843 scout southern road from Willamette Valley, through Umpqua, Rogue, and Klamath basins, across northern Nevada to Ft. Hall (Pocatello) and lead first immigrant wagons back over Applegate Trail.

President Polk approves military posts along Oregon Trail.

1847 Whitmans and 11 others murdered at Waiilatpu by Cayuse Indians; Lapwai mission abandoned by Spaldings. Three decades of Indian-white conflict begins.

1848 Congress organizes Oregon Territory.

Gold discovery in California lures away more than half of able-bodied men, leaving businesses, farms, and families; results in excellent markets for raw and finished products; sends first wagon trains from Oregon into California; and brings flow of gold as medium of exchange to bolster economy.

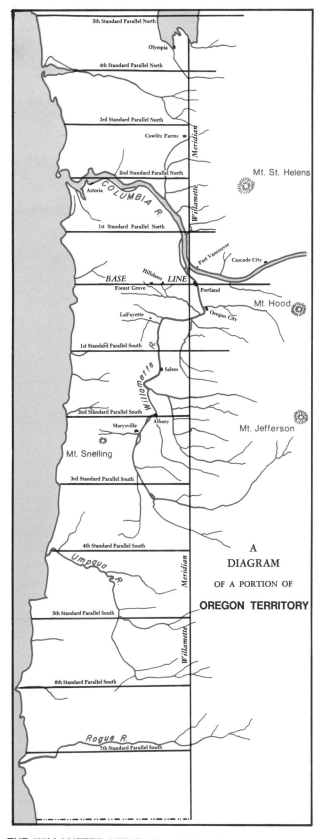

THE WILLAMETTE MERIDIAN and base line, from "A Diagram of a Portion of Oregon Territory." Surveyor-General's Office, 1851

Two Centuries of Development   9

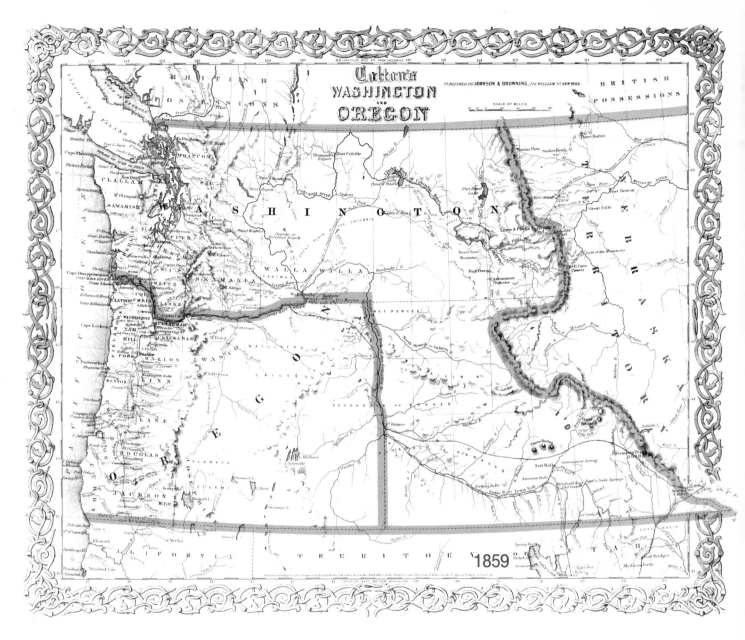

1849 Beaver Money, $5 and $10 solid gold pieces, coined by provisional government.

Joseph Lane, appointed by President Polk, installed as first territorial governor; legislature meets at Oregon City.

U.S. Army builds Fort Steilacoom on Puget Sound to protect settlers from Indians.

1850 Donation Land Claim law passed by Congress, enabling old and new settlers to obtain clear title to property; provides a catalyst to further immigration.

Territorial legislature moves capital to Salem.

Steamboat *Columbia* launched at Astoria and begins regular service between Astoria and Oregon City.

1851 Convention at Cowlitz Prairie asks Congress to form separate territory north of the Columbia.

Denny pioneer party arrives at Alki Point (Seattle).

Portland (named for Portland, Maine) incorporated.

1851-65 Gold discovery, at first in southern Oregon on fork of Illinois River and Jackson and Josephine creeks, and through the 1850's and 1860's in eastern Oregon (Auburn, Canyon City, Baker, Powder River), in Idaho (Oro Fino, Pierce City, Elk City, Florence, Idaho City, Silver City, Ruby City), and Washington (Old Fort Colville, Okanogan, Wenatchee) leads to

"rushes" across the region, only partly hampered by Indians opposing incursions on their lands; boom towns spring up; outfitting centers such as Portland, The Dalles, Walla Walla, and Lewiston do big business.

1852 Bellingham, Tacoma settled; Seattle platted.

The Monticello Convention—at present Longview—and *The Columbian,* first Washington newspaper—published at Olympia—advocate new territory north of Columbia.

Large immigration across plains to Pacific Northwest.

1853 President Fillmore signs bill creating Washington Territory—present states of Washington, Idaho, and parts of Montana and Wyoming with a white population of 3,965.

President Pierce appoints Isaac I. Stevens, Army engineer, as territorial governor of Washington, superintendent of Indian affairs, and chief of transcontinental railroad surveys between the 47th and 49th parallels.

Stevens begins surveys enroute to Olympia; his assistant, Capt. G. B. McClellan, surveys Cascade passes.

Jacksonville founded; Rogue River valley purchased from Indians for $60,000.

1854 Washington Territorial Legislature meets at Olympia. Oregon statehouse built in Salem.

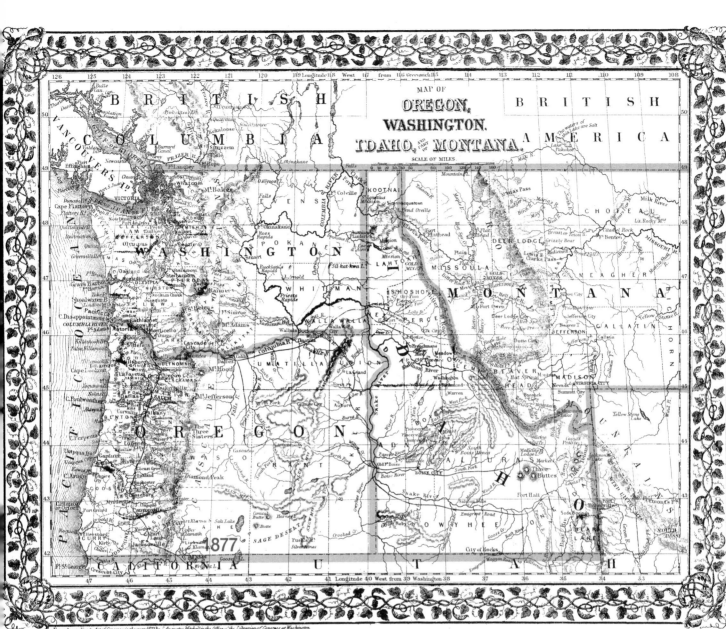

Treaties negotiated with Puget Sound Indians but conflicts continue in Idaho.

1855 Mormons from Utah settle in Lemhi Valley, Idaho; build canals for irrigation.

Indian wars cause Stevens to close eastern Washington to settlement.

1855-56 Stevens succeeds in making treaties with some tribes.

1856 Siege of Bradford's store at Cascade Rapids and other Indian troubles cause HBC to close Ft. Boise and Ft. Hall.

U.S. Army builds Forts Yamhill, Hoskins, and Umpqua in Oregon Coast Range to contain Indians, mostly from Rogue Valley, on coastal reservations.

1856-62 First railroad, beginning as a tramway, built as portage around rapids in Columbia Gorge; **Oregon Pony,** first steam locomotive in region, put into use on 14-mile narrow-gage railroad.

1857 Stevens sent to Congress to represent Washington Territory.

Congress grants Northern Pacific charter to build railroad from Great Lakes to Pacific north of 45th parallel.

Oregon ratifies state constitution.

1858 Mormons abandon Lemhi because of Indian troubles. Col. George Wright defeats Indians and eastern Washington reopened to settlement.

1859 Oregon becomes 33rd state; John Whiteaker elected governor.

Ladd and Tilden open first bank in Oregon at Portland.
San Juan Islands dispute becomes acute.

1859-62 Mullan Military Road built through northern **Idaho** from Ft. Benton on the Missouri to Ft. Walla Walla on the Columbia.

1860 Mormons make first permanent settlement in Idaho **at** Franklin.

Daily stage coach service established between Portland **and** Sacramento.

1860-62 Oregon Steam Navigation Co. nearly monopolizes steamboat travel on Columbia.

1861 First Oregon Cavalry and ten companies of Washington volunteers enlist for Civil War duty, stationed throughout region to man federal forts and to protect settlements and wagon trains from Indians.

Lewiston becomes first city incorporated in Idaho.

Two Centuries of Development   11

	Oregon	Washington	Idaho
1850	12,093	1,201	
1860	52,465	11,594*	
1870	90,923	23,955	17,804
1880	174,768	75,116	32,610
1890	317,704	357,232	88,548
1900	413,536	518,103	161,772
1910	672,765	1,141,990	325,594
1920	783,389	1,356,621	431,866
1930	953,786	1,563,396	445,032
1940	1,089,684	1,736,191	524,873
1950	1,521,341	2,378,963	588,637
1960	1,768,687	2,853,214	667,191
1970	2,091,385	3,409,169	712,567

* All of Washington Territory, including present state of Idaho and parts of Montana and Wyoming.

1862 National Homestead Act encourages settlement.
First Idaho newspaper *Golden Age*, published at Lewiston.
La Grande founded; Grande Ronde and Boise valley settled.
Vigilance Committee created at Salmon River mines.
Former Governor (General) Stevens killed in battle in Virginia.

1863 Congress organizes Idaho Territory; William Wallace appointed governor; legislature meets at Lewiston.
Boise Barracks established and city of Boise laid out.
Lewiston Vigilance Committee punishes robbers.

1864 Transcontinental telegraph connection completed into Portland via California.
Fort Stevens built at mouth of Columbia.
"Mercer Girls"—Civil War orphans and widows—brought to Seattle by Asa Mercer, find husbands available.
Payette Vigilance Committee formed to rid area of horse thieves and gold-dust counterfeiters.
Idaho capital moved from Lewiston to Boise.
Ben Holladay contracts to carry U.S. mail between Salt Lake City and The Dalles, via Boise and Walla Walla.

1865 First National Bank of Portland organized.

1866 More "Mercer Girls" arrive in Seattle.

1867 Washington legislature asks Congress to create new state.
Puget Sound ports recognized as closest U.S. ports to new territory when Alaska purchased from Russia.

1867-68 Cargoes of wheat shipped directly to Australia and England.

1868-1909 Railroads Three companies organized (1866-68) to obtain federal land grants and build railroads from Portland south through Willamette Valley and on to California. Ben Holladay, stage line operator, gains control, completes 20 miles in 1869, and on to Roseburg in 1872 with aid of land grants and bonds sold in Germany. Northern Pacific builds from Kalama on Columbia to Tacoma 1870-73. D. S. Baker, Walla Walla banker, builds railroad from Wallula to Walla Walla 1872-75. In 1874, Henry Villard, representing bondholders, comes from Germany. He gains control of Holladay interests in 1876, of steamship lines on the Columbia from German bankers in 1879, and the whole Northern Pacific Company in 1881. NP finishes line from St. Paul to Spokane (1881), to Wallula connecting by new line along south bank of Columbia to Portland in 1883. Then Villard empire collapses, mainly because roads run through unsettled areas which do not produce enough income to pay interest on debts. But building continues. Oregon line extends to Ashland in 1884, over Siskiyous to California in 1887. Utah and Northern comes into Idaho in 1877; Union Pacific crosses state in 1882 and with E. H. Harriman in control builds many branch lines. First train from Omaha to Portland 1885. NP crosses Cascades to Tacoma 1887. Great Northern builds across northern Idaho and Washington to Seattle in 1892; Chicago, Milwaukee, and St. Paul to Tacoma in 1909. Many branch lines completed throughout region in 40-year period. See map on page 26.

1870 Range and cattle business begins in Idaho on small scale.

D. S. Baker starts first bank in Washington Territory at Walla Walla.

1871 Rev. Spalding reopens Lapwai mission, but it closes upon his death in 1874; site now headquarters of Nez Percé National Historical Park.

1871-72 Dispute over ownership of San Juan Island between U.S. and Great Britain arbitrated by Emperor William I of Germany and settled in favor of U.S.

1872-73 Modoc War ends with capture of Captain Jack's band.

1874-75 Telegraph lines extended from Winnemucca, Nevada, to Silver City and Boise, Idaho.

1877 After Nez Percé War, Chief Joseph surrenders, declaring, "I will fight no more forever," and is sent to southern Kansas.

1879 Fort Coeur d'Alene established.

1884-85 Lead and silver mines discovered in what has become the fabulously rich Coeur d'Alene district in north Idaho.

1889 Washington becomes 42nd state, with Elisha P. Ferry the first governor and Olympia the capital.

1890 Idaho admitted as 43rd state, with George L. Shoup first governor and Boise City the capital.

1890-1900 "Apple fever" draws many fruit and berry growers, especially to Wenatchee, Hood River, and Rogue River valleys.

1891 Puget Sound Navy Yard located at Bremerton.

1892-1909 Labor disputes in Coeur d'Alene district, involving federal troops, murder of an ex-governor, and trial of labor leaders draw international attention.

1896 Transpacific steamship service inaugurated by Nippon Yusen Kaisya from Japan to Puget Sound.

1897 Gold rush to the Klondike begins; as principal outfitting and shipping center, Seattle grows rapidly.

1898 Several thousand men enlist for Spanish-American War duty.

1899 Mt. Rainier National Park created.

20th Century

In the 20th century, development of the region continued at an even more accelerated pace. Road and highways, stage coach lines, railroads with freight and passenger service crisscrossed the region. Promotional campaigns by railroad companies and land developers and large expositions in Portland (1905) and Seattle (1909) brought many international visitors. Settlement spread and population increased (see table). Lumbering, agriculture, and other industries expanded massively, especially in times of national need such as during World Wars I and II. Management of water resources resulted in huge irrigation and reclamation projects, better land use through flood control, and creation of large amounts of electrical energy, attracting new industries. Improving transportation—opening of the Panama Canal, clearing waterways and building port facilities, establishing air passenger and freight service within and beyond the region, constructing high-speed freeways—provided foundation for a broad economic base.

Today the Pacific Northwest and its resources have reached the state of development depicted in the following chapters.

Useful References on Place Names

Oregon Geographic Names by Lewis A. MacArthur. Portland: Binfords and Mort, 1952.

Washington State Place Names by James W. Phillips. Seattle: University of Washington Press, 1972.

Twenty-Third Biennial Report of the Idaho State Historical Department 1951-52

Origin of Washington Geographic Names by Edmond S. Meany. Seattle: University of Washington Press, 1923.

Early Colleges and Universities of the Pacific Northwest

Those founded before 1900 in order of chartering or establishment

Present name	Founded as	Year	First instruction at college level	First baccalaureate degree
Willamette University ..	Oregon Institute	1842	1853	1859
Pacific University	Tualatin Academy	1849	1854	1863
Linfield College	Oregon City Col.	1849	1865	1870
Oregon C of Education ..	Monmouth University	1856	1861	1942
Oregon State University..	Corvallis College	1858	1865	1870
Whitman College	Whitman College	1859	1882	1886
Univ of Washington	Terr Univ of Wash	1861	1861	1876
Lewis and Clark College	Albany College	1867	1867	1873
University of Oregon	University of Oregon	1872	1876	1878
George Fox College	Friends Pacific Acad	1885	1891	1892
Mt. Angel Seminary	Mt. Angel College	1887	1887	1893
Gonzaga University	Gonzaga College	1887	1890	1894
Mt. Angel College	Mt. Angel Normal Sch	1887	1892	1936
Univ. of Puget Sound ..	Puget Sound Univ	1888	1890	1893
University of Idaho	University of Idaho	1889	1892	1896
Central Wash St Col ..	State Normal School	1890	1891	1933
Eastern Wash St Col ..	State Normal School	1890	1890	1933
Pacific Lutheran Univ ..	Pacific Lutheran U	1890	1894	
Washington State Univ..	State Agric Col	1890	1892	1897
Whitworth College	Whitworth College	1890	1890	1896
College of Idaho	College of Idaho	1891	1906	1911
Seattle Pacific Col	Seattle Seminary	1891	1910	1915
Seattle University	Seattle College	1891	1900	1909
Walla Walla College	Walla Walla College	1892	1892	1909
Marylhurst College	St. Mary's Acad & Col	1893	1894	1898
Western Wash St Col ..	St Normal School	1893	1899	1933
Northwest Christian C..	Eugene Divinity Sch	1895	1895	1899
St. Martin's College	junior college	1895	1900	1940

Origin of Names of Oregon Counties

County and county seat	Date established	Origin of name of county
Baker, Baker	1862	E. D. Baker, US Senator, Oregon
Benton, Corvallis	1847	T. H. Benton, US Senator, Missouri
Clackamas, Oregon City	1843	Clackamas Indians
Clatsop, Astoria	1844	Clatsop Indians
Columbia, St. Helens	1854	Columbia River, for Gray's ship
Coos, Coquille	1853	*Koo'as, Kowes, Koos,* or *Coose* Indians
Crook, Prineville	1882	George Crook, Major General, US Army
Curry, Gold Beach	1855	G. L. Curry, territorial governor
Deschutes, Bend	1916	French *Riviere des Chutes*
Douglas, Roseburg	1852	Stephen A. Douglas, US Senator, Illinois
Gilliam, Condon	1885	Cornelius Gilliam, colonel, Cayuse War, 1848
Grant, Canyon City	1864	Ulysses S. Grant, General, US Army
Harney, Burns	1889	Wm. S. Harney, Major General, US Army
Hood River, Hood River	1908	Hood River, fr. Mt. Hood, fr. Lord Hood
Jackson, Medford	1852	Andrew Jackson, US President
Jefferson, Madras	1914	Mt. Jefferson, fr. Thomas Jefferson
Josephine, Grants Pass....	1856	Josephine Rollins, 1st white woman resident
Klamath, Klamath Falls	1882	Klamath Indians
Lake, Lakeview	1874	Many lakes in county
Lane, Eugene	1851	Joseph Lane, first territorial governor
Lincoln, Newport	1893	Abraham Lincoln, US President
Linn, Albany	1847	L. F. Linn, US Senator, Missouri
Malheur, Vale	1887	French *River au Malheur*
Marion, Salem	1843	F. Marion, General, Revolutionary War
Morrow, Heppner	1885	J. L. Morrow, early resident
Multnomah County	1854	Multnomah Indians
Polk, Dallas	1845	James K. Polk, US President
Sherman, Moro	1889	Wm. T. Sherman, General, US Army
Tillamook, Tillamook	1853	Tillamook Indians
Umatilla, Pendleton	1862	Umatilla River, Indian name
Union, La Grande	1864	Town of Union founded during Civil War
Wallowa, Enterprise	1887	Indian word for fish trap
Wasco, The Dalles	1854	Wasco (or *Wascopam*) Indians
Washington, Hillsboro	1843	George Washington, US President
Wheeler, Fossil	1899	Henry Wheeler, stage line operator
Yamhill, McMinnville	1843	Yamhill River, fr. Yamhill Indians

Origin of Names of Idaho Counties

County and county seat	Date established	Origin of name of county
Ada, Boise	1864	Ada Riggs, first white child born in Boise
Adams, Council	1911	John Adams, US President
Bannock, Pocatello	1893	Bannock Indians
Bear Lake, Paris	1875	Black bears in vicinity
Benewah, St. Maries	1915	Coeur d'Alene chief
Bingham, Blackfoot	1885	H. H. Bingham, US Congressman, Pennsylvania
Blaine, Hailey	1895	James G. Blaine, US Senator
Boise, Idaho City	1864	Fr. French for "wooded" river
Bonner, Sandpoint	1907	E. L. Bonner, early ferryman
Bonneville, Idaho Falls ..	1911	B. L. E. de Bonneville, Capt., US Army
Boundary, Bonners Ferry	1915	On the Canadian boundary
Butte, Arco	1917	Big Butte, landmark on Oregon Trail
Camas, Fairfield	1917	Camas plant; "sweet" in Chinook
Canyon, Caldwell	1891	Local canyon
Caribou, Soda Springs	1919	"Cariboo" Fairchild, early miner
Cassia, Burley	1879	Fr. French word for "raft"
Clark, Dubois	1919	Sam Clark, early settler
Clearwater, Orofino	1911	*Kookooskia,* Indian for "clear water"
Custer, Challis	1881	G. A. Custer, General, US Army
Elmore, Mountain Home	1889	Elmore mine at Rocky Bar
Franklin, Preston	1913	Franklin D. Richards of Utah
Fremont, St. Anthony	1893	J. C. Fremont, explorer and surveyor
Gem, Emmett	1915	Idaho nickname, "gem state"
Gooding, Gooding	1913	Frank Gooding, former Idaho governor
Idaho, Grangeville	1851	Steamer *Idaho* used by miners
Jefferson, Rigby	1913	Thomas Jefferson, US President
Jerome, Jerome	1919	Jerome Hill
Kootenai, Coeur d'Alene	1864	*Kutenai* Indian tribe
Latah, Moscow	1888	Latah Creek
Lemhi, Salmon	1869	King Limhi in *Book of Mormon*
Lewis, Nezperce	1911	M. Lewis, Lewis and Clark expedition
Lincoln, Shoshone	1895	Abraham Lincoln, US President
Madison, Rexburg	1913	James Madison, US President
Minidoka, Rupert	1913	Dakota word for spring or well
Nez Perce, Lewiston	1861	French "pierced nose"
Oneida, Malad	1864	Oneida, New York
Owyhee, Murphy	1863	Old spelling of "Hawaii"
Payette, Payette	1917	F. Payette, Hudson's Bay Co. trapper
Power, American Falls	1913	Power plant at American Falls
Shoshone, Wallace	1858	Shoshoni Indians
Teton, Driggs	1915	Teton peaks, Wyoming
Twin Falls, Twin Falls ..	1907	Falls on Snake River
Valley, Cascade	1917	Valley of Payette River
Washington, Weiser	1879	George Washington, US President

Origin of Names of Washington Counties

County and county seat	Date established	Origin of name of county
Adams, Ritzville	1883	John Adams, US President
Asotin, Asotin	1883	Nez Perce Indians
Benton, Prosser	1905	T. H. Benton, US Senator, Missouri
Chelan, Wenatchee	1899	Indian "deep water," Lake Chelan
Clallam, Port Angeles	1854	Nusklaim Indians
Clark, Vancouver	1849	W. Clark, Lewis and Clark Expedition
Columbia, Dayton	1895	Columbia River, fr. Gray's ship
Cowlitz, Kelso	1854	Cowlitz Indians
Douglas, Waterville	1883	S. A. Douglas, US Senator, Illinois
Ferry, Republic	1899	E. P. Ferry, first Washington governor
Franklin, Pasco	1883	Benjamin Franklin, colonial statesman
Garfield, Pomeroy	1881	James A. Garfield, US President
Grant, Ephrata	1909	Ulysses S. Grant, US President
Grays Harbor, Montesano	1854	Robert Gray, US explorer
Island, Coupeville	1853	Consists solely of islands
Jefferson, Port Townsend	1852	Thomas Jefferson, US President
King, Seattle	1852	W. R. D. King, US Senator, Ala.
Kitsap, Port Orchard	1857	War chief and medicine man
Kittitas, Ellensburg	1883	K'tatas Indians
Klickitat, Goldendale	1859	Klickitat Indians
Lewis, Chehalis	1845	M. Lewis, Lewis and Clark Expedition
Lincoln, Davenport	1883	Abraham Lincoln, US President
Mason, Shelton	1854	C. H. Mason, first secretary, Wash. terr.
Okanogan, Okanogan	1888	Okanogan Indians
Pacific, South Bend	1851	Pacific Ocean
Pend Oreille, Newport	1911	French *pendant d'oreille,* "ear bobs"
Pierce, Tacoma	1852	Franklin Pierce, US President
San Juan, Friday Harbor	1873	Named in 1791 by Spanish
Skagit, Mount Vernon ..	1883	Skagit Indians
Skamania, Stevenson	1854	Indian "swift water," Columbia
Snohomish, Everett	1890	Snohomish Indians
Spokane, Spokane	1858	Spokane Indians
Stevens, Colville	1863	I. I. Stevens, first terr. governor
Thurston, Olympia	1852	S. R. Thurston, Oregon's first delegate to Congress
Wahkiakum, Cathlamet	1854	Kathlamet Indian village
Walla Walla, Walla W...	1854	Nez Perce and Cayuse Indians
Whatcom, Bellingham....	1854	Nooksack Indian Chief
Whitman, Colfax	1871	Dr. Marcus Whitman, missionary
Yakima, Yakima	1865	Yakima Indians

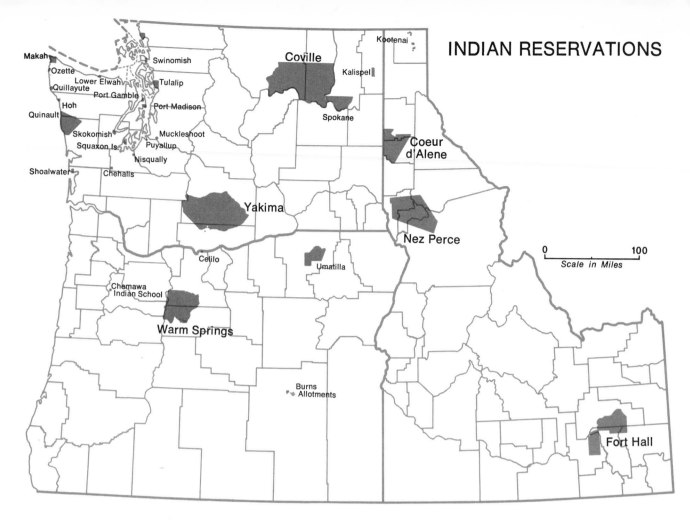

Burns Colony: Warm Springs Agency
11,786 acres; 129 Paiute Indians; 11,014 acres in Public Domain Allotments (grazing land) plus 606 acres submarginal and 166 acres homestead and homesite land; established 1934.

Chehalis Reservation: Western Washington Agency
1,682 acres; 441 Chehalis, Chinook, and Clatsop Indians; 1,393 forest land acreage; established 1864.

Coeur d'Alene Reservation: Northern Idaho Agency
69,300 acres; 483 Coeur d'Alene Indians; 29,807 forest land acreage, 5,177 open grazing land; established 1867.

Colville Reservation: Colville Agency
1,003,444 acres; 2,732 Colville Indians; 810,198 forest land acreage, 2,302 Public Domain (812,500 total), 146,981 open grazing land, 1,250 Public Domain (148,231 total); established 1872.

Ft. Hall Reservation: Ft. Hall Agency
482,066 acres; 3,038 Indians; 63,230 forest land acreage; 346,453 open grazing land, 2,204 private irrigation development (348,657 total); established 1868.

Hoh Reservation: Western Washington Agency
443 acres; 60 Indians; 438 forest land acreage; established 1893.

Kalispel Reservation: Northern Idaho Agency
4,558 acres; 128 Kalispel Indians; 2,540 forest land acreage, 1,783 open grazing land; established 1914.

Kootenai Reservation: Northern Idaho Agency
2,387 acres; 50 Kootenai Indians; 355 forest land acreage, 1,143 open grazing land; established 1894.

Lower Elwah Reservation: Western Washington Agency
372 acres; 250 Indians; Sec. Order to Purchase Reservation 1936.

Lummi Reservation: Western Washington Agency
7,016 acres; 1,225 Lummi Indians; 3,716 forest land acreage; established 1873.

Makah or Neah Bay Reservation: Western Washington Agency
27,024 acres; 805 Makah and Quileute Indians; 25,421 forest land acreage, 237 open grazing land; established 1855.

Muckleshoot Reservation: Western Washington Agency
1,189 acres; 531 Muckleshoot Indians; 889 forest land acreage; established 1857.

Nez Perce or Lapwai Reservation: Northern Idaho Agency
87,660 acres; 1,303 Nez Perce Indians; 28,734 forest land acreage; 23,869 open grazing land; established 1895.

Nisqually Reservation: Western Washington Agency
1,111 acres; 85 Nisqually Indians; 761 forest land acreage; 72 open grazing land; established 1857.

Ozette Reservation: Western Washington Agency
719 acres being held in trust for use and benefit of Makah Tribe; the Ozette Indians abandoned the land; 719 forest land acreage; established 1893.

Port Gamble: Western Washington Agency
1,301 acres; 300 Clallam Indians; 1,169 forest land acreage; established 1938.

Port Madison Reservation: Western Washington Agency
2,680 acres; 177 Suquamish Indians; 2,333 forest land acreage; established 1855.

Puyallup Reservation: Western Washington Agency
35 acres; 450 Puyallup Indians; established 1854.

Quillayute Reservation: Western Washington Agency
837 acres; 450 Quileute Indians; 577 forest land acreage; established 1855.

Quinault Reservation: Western Washington Agency
128,028 acres; 1,200 Quinault Indians; 127,300 forest land acreage; established 1855.

Shoalwater Reservation: Western Washington Agency
1,682 acres; 12 Lower Chehalis Indians; 329 forest land acreage; established 1866.

Skokomish Reservation: Western Washington Agency
2,921 acres; 386 Skokomish, Clallam and Twana Indians; 2,837 forest land acreage; established 1855.

Spokane Reservation: Spokane Agency
137,150 acres; 1,650 Spokane Indians; 106,973 forest land acreage; 23,486 open grazing land, 175 Public Domain (23,661 total); established 1881.

Squaxin Island Reservation: Western Washington Agency
1,416 acres; 157 Squaxin Indians; 828 forest land acreage; established 1855.

Swinomish Reservation: Western Washington Agency
3,370 acres; 495 Swinomish Indians; 3,076 forest land acreage; established 1873.

Tulalip Reservation (Snohomish): Western Washington Agency
9,128 acres; 950 Snohomish Indians; 7,237 forest land acreage; established 1873.

Umatilla Reservation: Umatilla Agency
86,278 acres; 1,410 Indians (Cayuse, Paiute, Umatilla, Walla Walla); 13,581 forest land acreage; 37,238 open grazing land; established 1855.

Warm Springs Reservation: Warm Springs Agency
564,330 acres; 1,930 Indians; 298,508 forest land acreage, 459 Dalles Public Domain Allotments (298,967 total); 182,266 open grazing land, 5,316 Dalles Public Domain Allotments (187,582 total); established 1855.

Yakima Reservation: Yakima Agency
1,095,261 acres; 5,897 Yakima Indians; 565,984 forest land acreage, 4,024 Columbia River Allotment (570,008 total); 432,052 open grazing land, 18,290 Public Domain (450,342 total); established 1855.

Source: Portland Area Office, Bureau of Indian Affairs, U. S. Department of Interior, July 1971.

14   Atlas of the Pacific Northwest

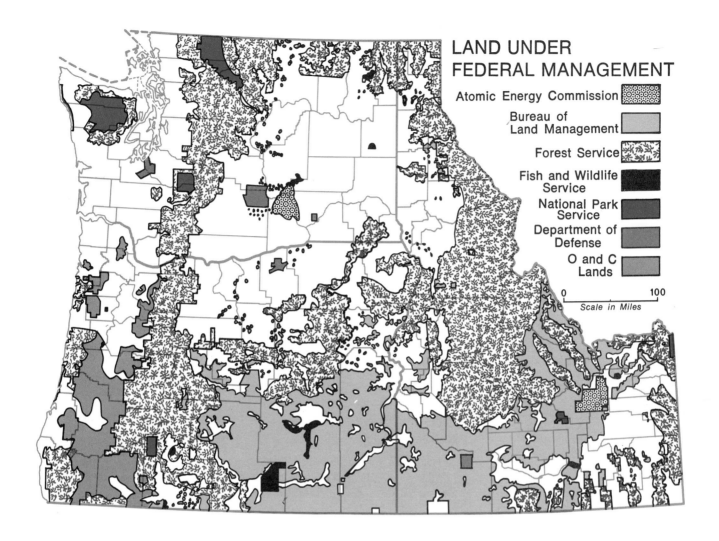

LAND UNDER
FEDERAL MANAGEMENT

Atomic Energy Commission

Bureau of
Land Management

Forest Service

Fish and Wildlife
Service

National Park
Service

Department of
Defense

O and C
Lands

0   100
Scale in Miles

PACIFIC NORTHWEST LANDS OWNED BY THE UNITED STATES GOVERNMENT

Agency	Oregon	Washington	Idaho	Total
	Acres	Acres	Acres	Acres
Department of Agriculture	15,477,304.9	9,044,359.7	20,384,618.3	44,906,282.9
Forest Service	(15,462,697.1)	(9,043,965.3)	(20,351,874.0)	(44,858,536.4)
Atomic Energy Commission		364,319.3	572,267.1	936,586.4
Department of Commerce	1,005.1	5.3		1,010.4
Department of Health, Education, and Welfare	1.4	27.4		28.8
Department of Interior	16,540,149.7	2,661,303.5	12,705,169.1	31,906,622.3
Bureau of Land Management	(15,687,642.0)	(293,067.0)	(12,113,193.4)	(28,093,902.4)
National Parks Service	(160,895.1)	(1,805,588.8)	(85,268.1)	(2,051,752.0)
Fish and Wildlife Service	(457,377.3)	(118,525.0)	(23,008.5)	(598,910.8)
O and C Lands	(2,638,945.0)			(2,638,945.0)
Department of Justice		4,420.7	4.1	4,424.8
Post Office Department	15.7	18.9	8.1	42.7
Department of Transportation	1,141.7	1,573.5	634.2	3,349.4
Veterans Administration	421.6	353.3	75.6	850.5
Department of of Defense	162,871.3	493,225.6	163,824.6	810,921.5
Total federal agencies	32,183,790.3	12,570,620.4	33,826,619.7	78,581,030.4
Total acreage of the states	61,598,720.0	'42,693,760.0	52,933,120.0	157,225,600.0
Owned by the federal government	52.2%	29.4%	63.9%	49.9%

SOURCE: Public Land Statistics, June 30, 1970

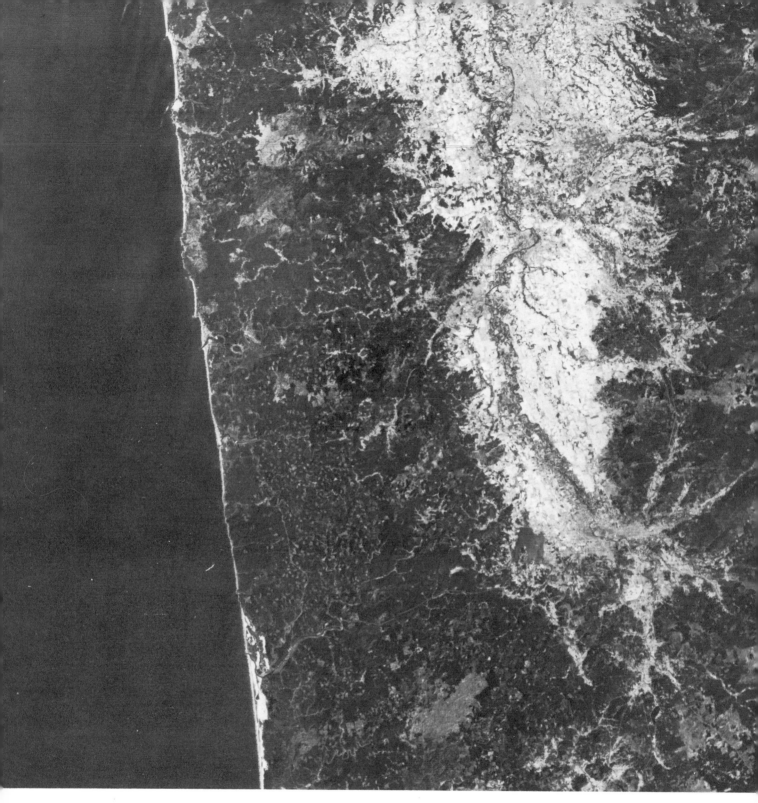

OREGON COAST from Cape Lookout south to Reedsport; Newport, Toledo, and Yaquina Bay near middle coast; heavily forested Coast Range; part of Willamette Valley from McMinnville south to Cottage Grove and Drain. Fern Ridge reservoir, dark gray rectangle southwest corner of valley. Cities (light gray): Eugene-Springfield, south end of valley; Corvallis-Albany, due east of Yaquina Bay; Salem, on right bank of Willamette toward top of photo. July 29, 1972.

COLUMBIA BASIN. The Snake River (top right) flows southwest into the Columbia River near Pasco and Kennewick. The Columbia (from top center) flows southeast and then west into the Columbia Gorge (left margin). It widens upriver behind the Priest Rapids Dam (top center), the McNary Dam (below mouth of the Snake), the John Day Dam, and The Dalles Dam (lower left). Dark orchards and irrigated farms of the Yakima Valley (upper center) contrast with dry wheat lands of Horse Heaven Hills (center) in this aerial photograph taken from an altitude of about 500 miles, October 7, 1972.

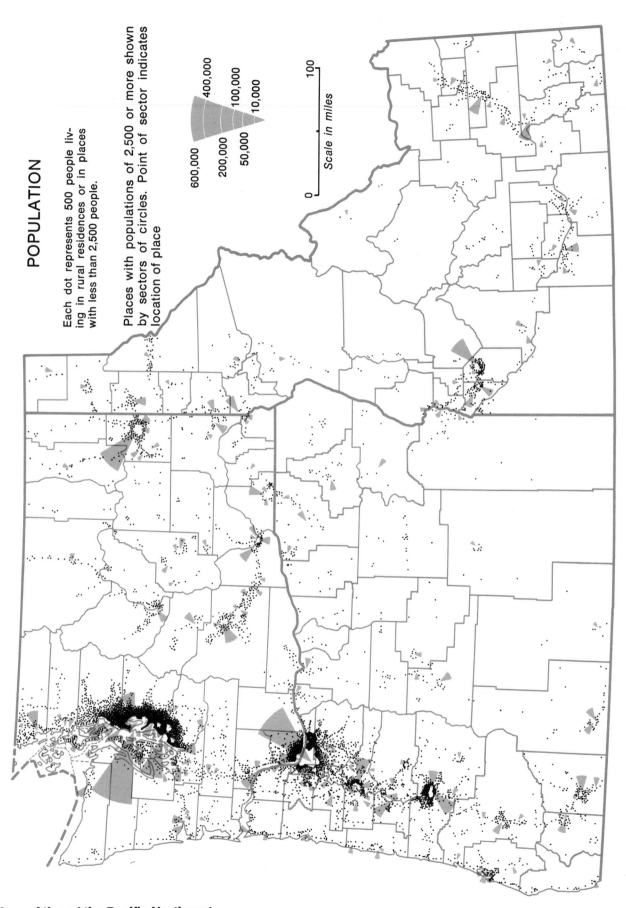

POPULATION

Each dot represents 500 people living in rural residences or in places with less than 2,500 people.

Places with populations of 2,500 or more shown by sectors of circles. Point of sector indicates location of place

600,000
400,000
200,000
100,000
50,000
10,000

Scale in miles

0   100

In 1970, the three states of the Pacific Northwest had a combined population of approximately 6.2 million, an increase of about one million over what it had been in 1960 and more than one and one-half million greater than the population in 1950. The projected population of the region to the year 2020 is 12.7 million, although this may not be realized if the current patterns of a slackening of in-migration and a lessening of birth rate continue.

At present, the Pacific Northwest includes about 3% of the national population, which is approximately the same proportion that resided in the region in 1960 and 1950. Of the states in the Pacific Northwest, Washington is the most populous, as it has been since 1890, and today includes about 55% of the regional total. Oregon contains about 34% and Idaho about 11% of the regional population.

Population density in the United States is approximately 58 persons per square mile; state densities in the Pacific Northwest are lower than the national average, with densities of 51, 22, and 9 in Washington, Oregon, and Idaho respectively. There are, however, considerable differences in population densities among counties in the Pacific Northwest, with densities of some counties west of the Cascade Mountains in excess of 250 per square mile. For the most part, the highest densities exist in the Puget Sound Lowland, the Willamette Valley, south-central Washington, and the Snake River Plain. By contrast, many counties east of the Cascades have densities of less than ten persons per square mile.

Population changes within the Pacific Northwest in past decades have often involved in-migration. This has slowed appreciably and now little more than offsets out-migration from the region. As noted earlier, however, there has been an increase in population, this coming more from natural reproduction than from in-migration.

Of major significance has been the redistribution of regional population involving migration among counties. Numerous counties in eastern Washington and Oregon and in northern Idaho have suffered population losses, at the same time, increases in county populations of western Washington and Oregon have exceeded the national average of all counties.

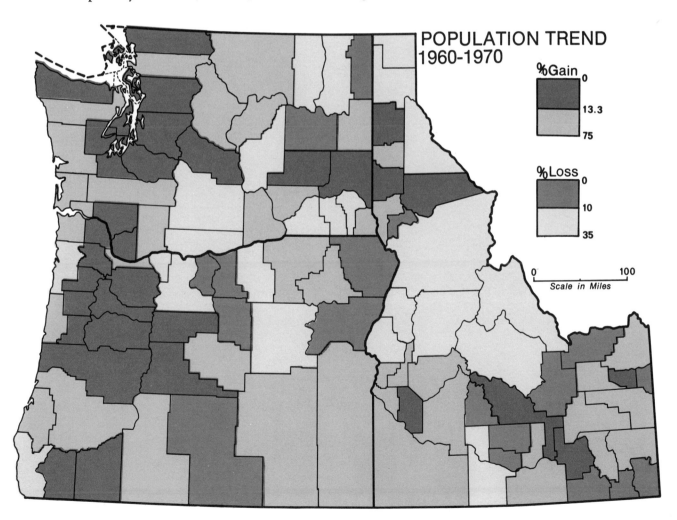

POPULATION TREND
1960-1970

%Gain 0
13.3
75

%Loss 0
10
35

0   100
Scale in Miles

POPULATION DENSITY 1970

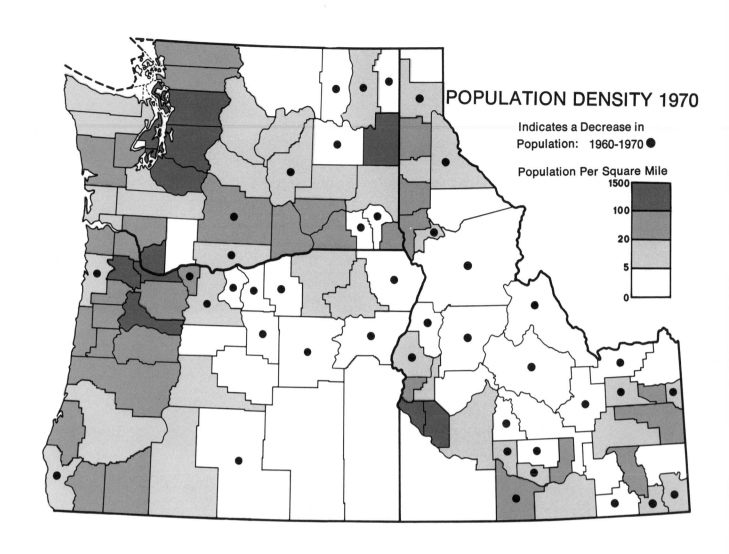

Indicates a Decrease in
Population: 1960-1970 ●

Population Per Square Mile

1500	
100	
20	
5	
0	

URBAN AND RURAL POPULATION 1900-1970

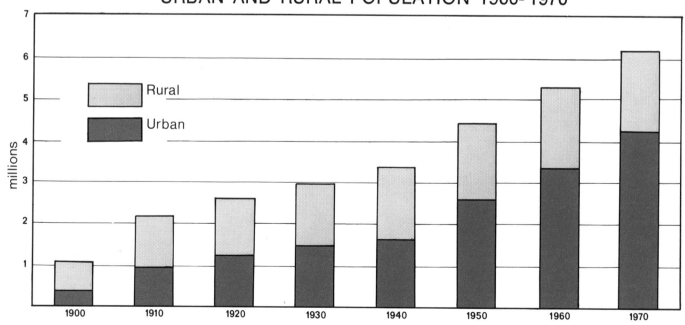

Rural

Urban

millions

1900 1910 1920 1930 1940 1950 1960 1970

Urbanization

Of the total population of the United States, 73.5% resides in urban centers; the urban population of each of the states in the Pacific Northwest is below this average. The urban populations of Washington, Oregon, and Idaho are 72.6, 67.1, and 54.1% respectively of state totals. Each of the states within the region has, however, become urbanized at rates greater than the national average in recent years.

By census definition, urban places are those containing 2,500 or more inhabitants. Not all places in the region that meet the criteria of "urban place" have experienced population increases in recent years. A number of smaller urban centers in eastern Washington and Oregon and in northern Idaho have suffered population losses in the past two or three decades. The larger urban centers and smaller ones in close proximity to major centers have experienced the greatest increases in population of late.

There are seven urbanized areas in the Pacific Northwest, and these include 53%, 51%, and 15% of the populations of Washington, Oregon, and Idaho respectively; collectively these areas contain 47% of the regional population. In the past decade, the central cities of urbanized areas have either slightly increased or as in the case of Seattle and Spokane, have lost population. By contrast, many smaller urban centers in the urban fringes, most of which are suburbs, have experienced the highest rates of growth of all urban centers in the region.

In summary, the greatest share of the population of the Pacific Northwest resides in urban centers, especially in the seven metropolitan areas of the region. The largest urban centers, however, are not the ones growing at the highest rates; this distinction is characteristic of urban centers within the urban fringes of metropolitan areas. Many smaller urban centers removed from the Willamette Valley and Puget Sound Lowland have had but modest population increases or have suffered population losses.

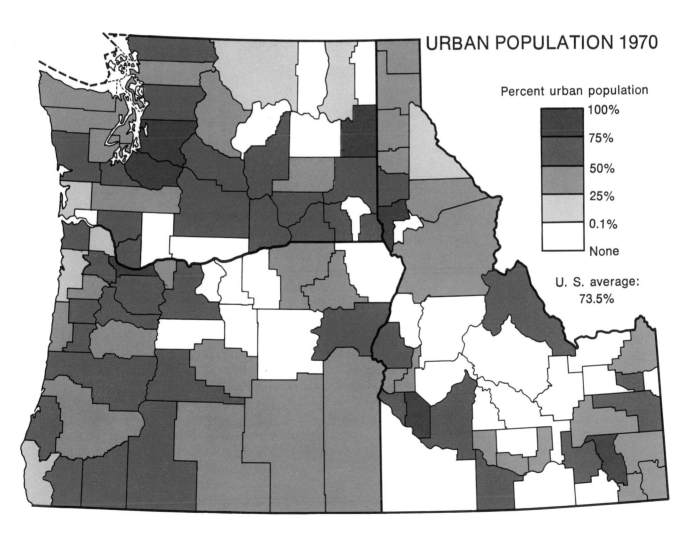

URBAN POPULATION 1970

Percent urban population

100%
75%
50%
25%
0.1%
None

U. S. average:
73.5%

Population inside and outside the Standard Metropolitan Statistical Areas (SMSA's)

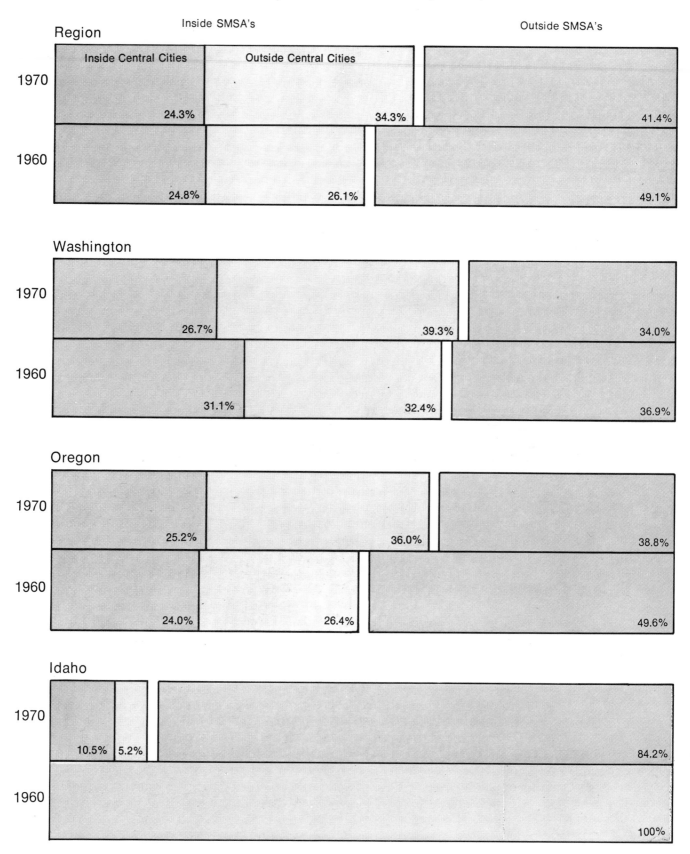

Inside SMSA's

Outside SMSA's

Region

Inside Central Cities | Outside Central Cities

1970 — 24.3% | 34.3% | 41.4%

1960 — 24.8% | 26.1% | 49.1%

Washington

1970 — 26.7% | 39.3% | 34.0%

1960 — 31.1% | 32.4% | 36.9%

Oregon

1970 — 25.2% | 36.0% | 38.8%

1960 — 24.0% | 26.4% | 49.6%

Idaho

1970 — 10.5% | 5.2% | 84.2%

1960 — 100%

Population by Size of Place 1970

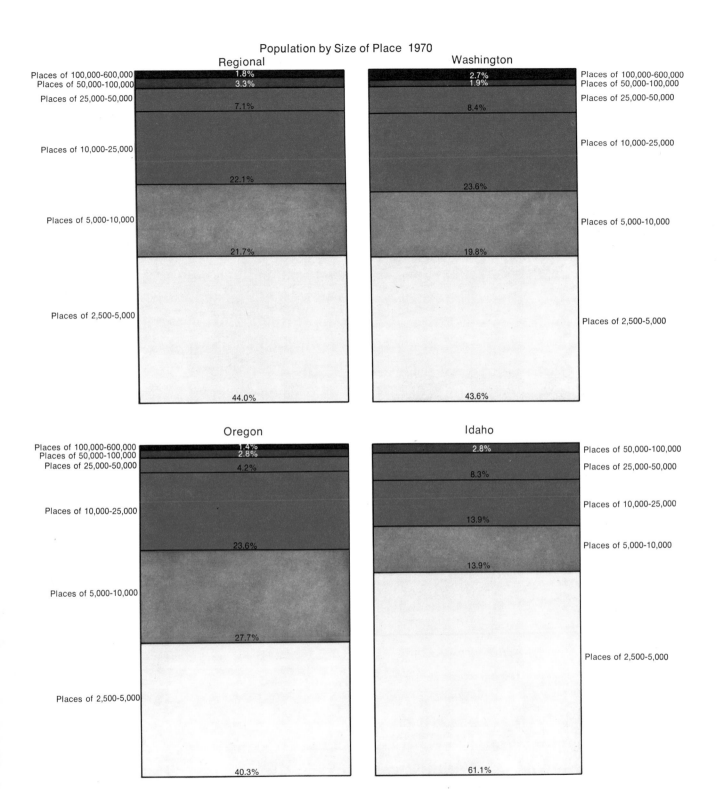

Regional

Places of 100,000-600,000 — 1.8%
Places of 50,000-100,000 — 3.3%
Places of 25,000-50,000 — 7.1%
Places of 10,000-25,000 — 22.1%
Places of 5,000-10,000 — 21.7%
Places of 2,500-5,000 — 44.0%

Washington

Places of 100,000-600,000 — 2.7%
Places of 50,000-100,000 — 1.9%
Places of 25,000-50,000 — 8.4%
Places of 10,000-25,000 — 23.6%
Places of 5,000-10,000 — 19.8%
Places of 2,500-5,000 — 43.6%

Oregon

Places of 100,000-600,000 — 1.4%
Places of 50,000-100,000 — 2.8%
Places of 25,000-50,000 — 4.2%
Places of 10,000-25,000 — 23.6%
Places of 5,000-10,000 — 27.7%
Places of 2,500-5,000 — 40.3%

Idaho

Places of 50,000-100,000 — 2.8%
Places of 25,000-50,000 — 8.3%
Places of 10,000-25,000 — 13.9%
Places of 5,000-10,000 — 13.9%
Places of 2,500-5,000 — 61.1%

Structure of labor force by state and economic sector, in 1960 and in 1970

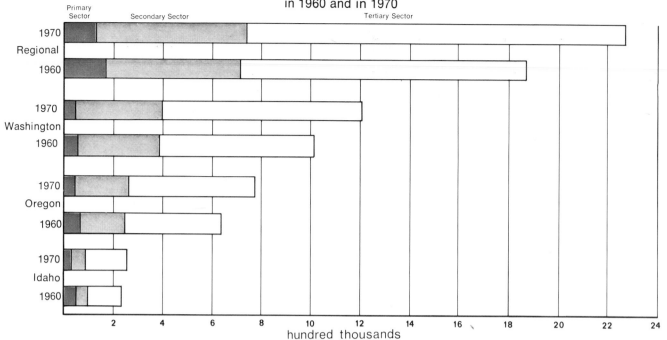

hundred thousands

Income of Employed Persons 14 years and over
(Median annual income)

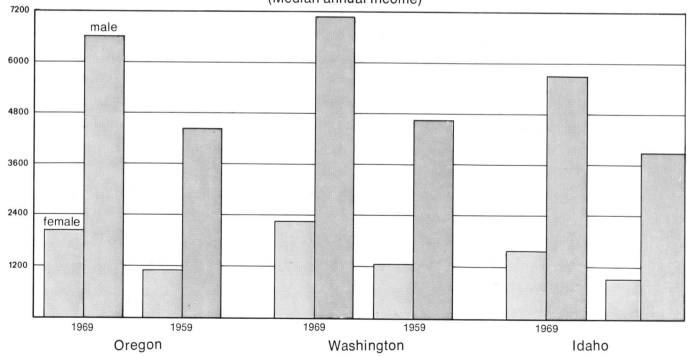

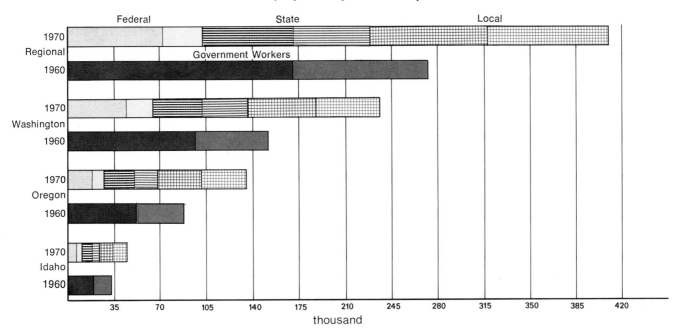

Public Employment by level and by state

Federal State Local

1970
Regional

Government Workers

1960

1970
Washington

1960

1970
Oregon

1960

1970
Idaho

1960

35 70 105 140 175 210 245 280 315 350 385 420

thousand

Labor Force

The labor force of the Pacific Northwest in 1970 was 2.3 million or 37% of the regional population. This compares with a regional labor force in 1960 of 1.9 million or 36% of the population. Of the total labor force in 1970, Washington accounted for 54%, Oregon 34%, and Idaho 11%. The state proportions of the regional labor force in 1960 were essentially what they were in 1970, indicating that state contributions to the regional labor force have been essentially unchanged in recent years.

The larbor force of the Pacific Northwest can be disaggregated into the primary, secondary, and tertiary sectors. The primary sector includes those economic activities based upon direct exploitation of the natural resource base, such as agriculture, forestry, commercial fishing, and mining. The secondary sector includes activities that utilize or process materials derived from the primary sector, specifically manufacturing and construction, while the tertiary sector includes those activities dealing with the distribution of goods and services, such as retail and wholesale trade, transportation, professional and personal services, and public administration.

Of the three economic sectors, the one most prominent in the labor force structure of the region and in each of the included states is the tertiary sector, which accounts for just over two-thirds of the regional labor force. This sector accounts for 68, 67, and 64% of the labor force in Washington, Oregon, and Idaho respectively. The secondary sector, which makes up slightly more than one-fourth of the regional labor force, accounts for one-fourth of the labor force in Washington and Oregon, but only about one-fifth in Idaho. In the region, the primary sector contributes about 6% of the labor force, with the proportion of 5%, 6%, and 15% of Washington, Oregon, and Idaho respectively.

Of special note is the role of public employment by different levels of government. Public employment accounted for 18% of the regional employment in 1970, an increase from 15% in 1960. Of total public employment in the region, local governments (counties and cities) accounted for 45% of the total in 1970, state governments 31%, and the federal government 24%. Further, this employment sector has exhibited considerable increases of late in the region and each of the included states, which is somewhat understandable when one notes that governments, especially the federal government, administer vast amounts of the land area of the region. (See table, page 15.)

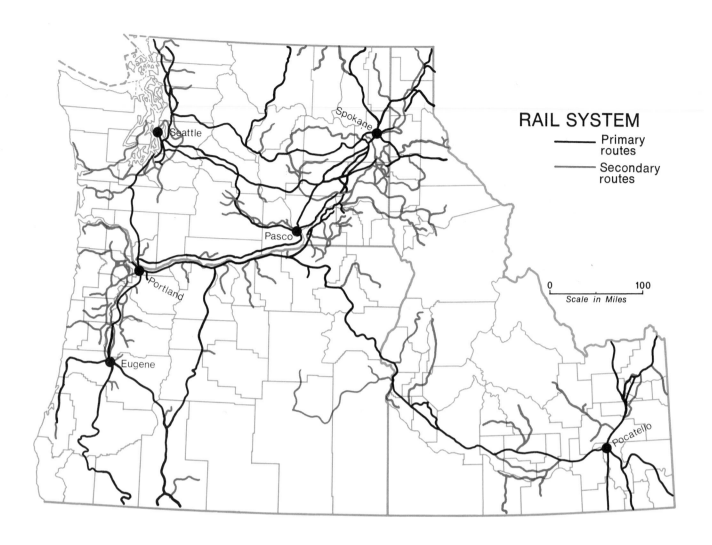

RAIL SYSTEM
—— Primary routes
—— Secondary routes

0   100
Scale in Miles

RAILROAD SHIPMENTS AND RECEIPTS BY STATE AND REGION

Tons of Revenue Freight Originated and Terminated
in the Pacific Northwest Region by Commodity Class, 1964

Commodity Classes	Idaho		Oregon		Washington		NWP Region	
	Orig.	Term	Orig.	Term	Orig.	Term	Orig.	Term
Lumber and wood products ..	24,165	9,735	142,149	34,022	61,441	52,532	227,755	96,289
Farm products	39,972	1,050	13,910	28,902	35,049	43,168	88,931	73,120
Food and kindred products ..	9,299	3,516	9,536	8,416	17,134	13,837	35,969	25,769
Pulp and paper products	--------	668	12,798	1,734	19,968	4,446	32,766	6,848
Non-metallic minerals	7,655	8,601	4,268	4,409	12,679	14,680	24,602	27,690
Primary metals	--------	2,125	3,688	5,824	7,569	9,665	11,257	17,614
Stone, clay, glass	--------	2,542	2,499	5,045	5,809	8,712	8,308	16,299
Petroleum and coal products	--------	1,854	4,396	4,487	3,200	4,902	7,596	11,243
Chemical and allied products	--------	3,700	922	5,180	5,169	8,276	6,091	17,156
Metallic ores	1,310	1,152	1,615	2,230	2,213	12,239	5,138	15,621
Unclassified	11,543	25,862	3,695	9,989	5,735	20,041	20,973	55,892
TOTALS	93,944	60,805	199,476	110,238	175,966	192,498	469,386	363,541

SOURCE: Interstate Commerce Commission, 1967

Transportation and Circulation _____ Ray M. Northam

TRANSPORTATION proved to be one of the factors most responsible for development of the Pacific Northwest, first in the form of sailing vessels plying the offshore waters and later by incursions into navigable waterways of Puget Sound and the Columbia River estuary. In the latter part of the 19th century, the Pacific Northwest was made more accessible to the rest of the country by the coming of the railroads, which not only served the coastal sections of the region, but facilitated settlement of the inland areas as well.

Today there is a well-developed system of transportation in the region with a fairly dense network of railroads and surfaced highways for the movement of commodities and people. Further, the Columbia River system has been improved so that barge traffic moves upstream from tidewater via the Columbia and Snake rivers as far as Lewiston, Idaho. The Columbia River, the only water level route through the Cascade Mountains into the interior of the region, has served as a major route not only for barge traffic but also for major highways and rail lines that follow closely the course of the river. Railroads and interstate freeways also provide linkages between the Pacific Northwest and the southwest, especially California.

The lower Columbia River serves as a major artery for ocean-going vessels engaged in coastwise shipping and foreign commerce, and efforts continue to maintain a 40-foot channel upstream to the confluence with the Willamette River. Ports on the lower Columbia River of significance to the region include Portland, Vancouver, and Astoria.

Puget Sound's deep-water harbors, especially those of Seattle, Tacoma, and Everett, accommodate modern merchant vessels, many of which are engaged in shipment of containerized cargoes. Major coastal ports are Coos Bay and Aberdeen, with a number of smaller ones of importance as well.

To serve the Pacific Northwest with modern forms of transportation, there is a fairly dense network of air routes scheduled for domestic and overseas flights, with overseas flights focusing upon international air terminals in Seattle-Tacoma and Portland. Further, the Pacific Northwest is served by pipelines bringing natural gas, crude oil, and refined products to the region from source areas in the southwestern U. S. and western Canada.

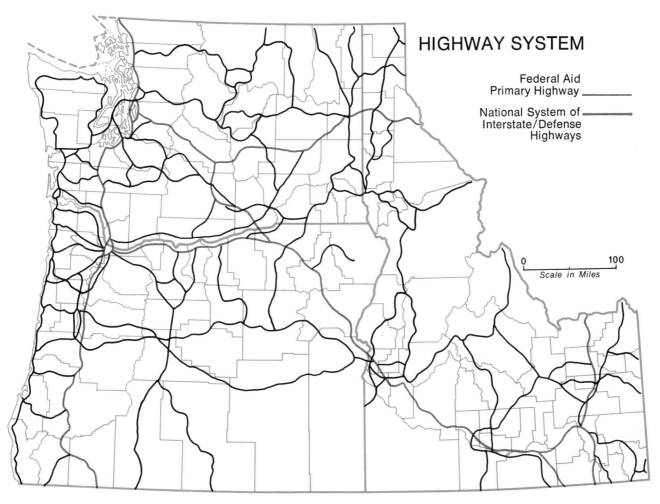

HIGHWAY SYSTEM

Federal Aid
Primary Highway _____

National System of _____
Interstate/Defense
Highways

0   100
Scale in Miles

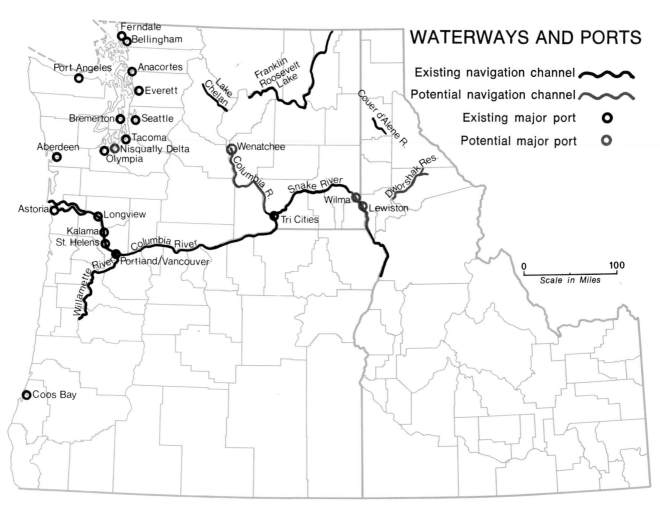

WATERWAYS AND PORTS

Existing navigation channel

Potential navigation channel

Existing major port ◎

Potential major port ◎

FREIGHT TRAFFIC THROUGH MAJOR PORTS, 1970
Short tons

| Port | Total | Foreign | | Domestic | | | | Local |
| | | Imports | Exports | Coastwise | | Internal | | |
				Receipts	Shipments	Receipts	Shipments	
Washington								
Grays Harbor and								
Chehalis River	3,574,467	4,498	2,143,432	188,410	64,216	409,918	2,323	761,670
Port Angeles Harbor	2,679,350	64,880	1,230,732	128,078	31,950	332,973	265,401	625,336
Port Townsend Harbor	1,169,238	223,491	21,670	23,775	na	641,947	258,355	na
Olympia Harbor	1,844,524	378	1,033,143	na	na	159,468	488,656	162,879
Tacoma Harbor	8,602,828	2,238,958	2,793,891	399,087	224,917	1,614,165	564,520	767,290
Seattle Harbor	15,247,524	2,654,516	1,684,913	2,174,030	875,382	5,762,645	1,630,480	465,558
Everett Harbor and								
Snokomish River	6,749,939	641,078	1,403,965	1,200	na	2,958,640	340,866	1,404,190
Anacortes Harbor	4,458,223	86,173	113,802	361,980	2,161,328	145,977	1,588,827	136
Bellingham Bay and Harbor	1,892,374	423,205	358,427	40,392	140,048	430,650	229,543	270,109
Port of Longview	5,884,082	451,992	3,116,840	674,760	197,423	1,105,275	76,452	261,340
Port of Kalama	1,205,777	11,636	805,338	20,340	na	261,913	106,550	na
Port of Vancouver	2,605,867	731,875	1,170,469	42,861	na	469,927	188,250	2,485
Oregon								
Port of Astoria	1,635,096	24,415	1,347,065	26,788	61,442	148,540	26,846	na
Port of Portland	15,490,354	1,322,296	3,885,865	4,420,624	308,888	2,864,114	1,117,662	1,570,905
Coos Bay	6,098,778	49	3,226,993	314,718	422,703	1,009,565	na	1,124,750

na = not available

SOURCE: Department of the Army, Corps of Engineers, *Waterborne Commerce of the United States*, 1970.

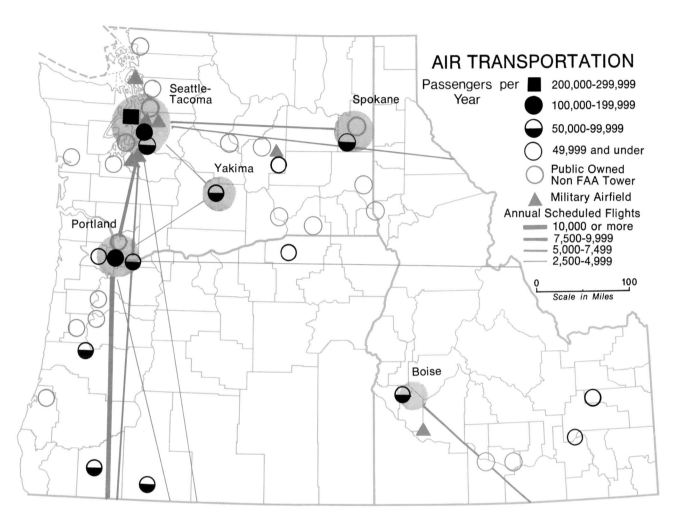

AIR TRANSPORTATION

Passengers per
Year

- ■ 200,000-299,999
- ● 100,000-199,999
- ◖ 50,000-99,999
- ○ 49,999 and under
- ○ Public Owned Non FAA Tower
- ▲ Military Airfield

Annual Scheduled Flights

- 10,000 or more
- 7,500-9,999
- 5,000-7,499
- 2,500-4,999

0   100
Scale in Miles

Seattle-Tacoma

Spokane

Yakima

Portland

Boise

AIR TRAFFIC HUBS*
Enplaned Passengers in the U.S.

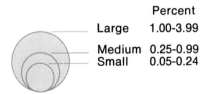

Percent

Large	1.00-3.99
Medium	0.25-0.99
Small	0.05-0.24

* An air traffic hub is a city or Standard Metropolitan Statistical Area; not an airport. Designation of a community as an air traffic hub is based on the community's share of the domestic air passenger market.

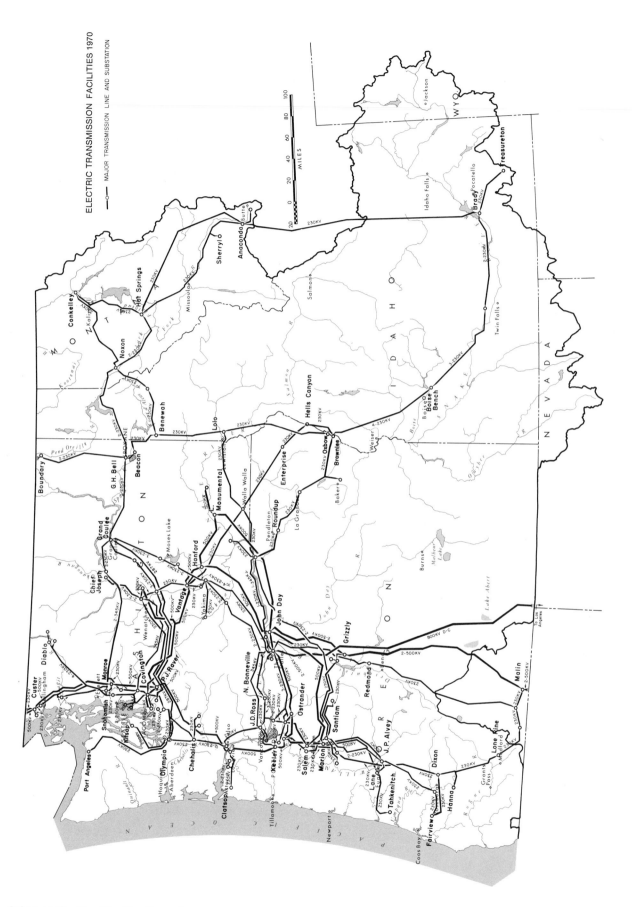

ELECTRIC TRANSMISSION FACILITIES 1970

— MAJOR TRANSMISSION LINE AND SUBSTATION

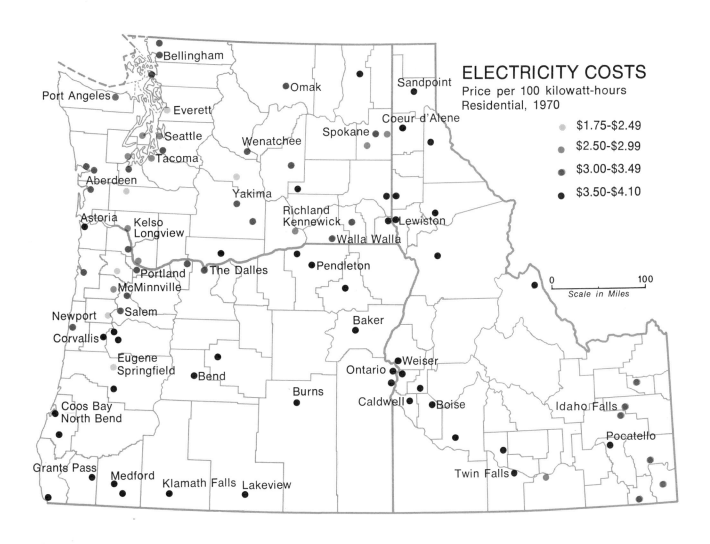

ELECTRICITY COSTS

Price per 100 kilowatt-hours
Residential, 1970

- $1.75-$2.49
- $2.50-$2.99
- $3.00-$3.49
- $3.50-$4.10

0   100
Scale in Miles

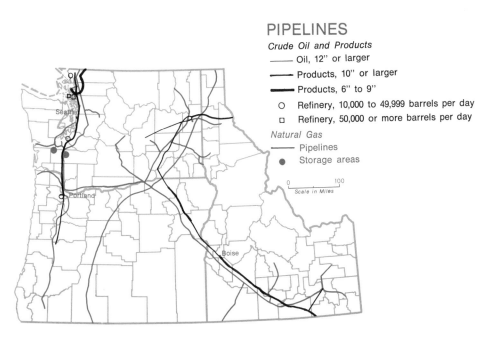

PIPELINES

Crude Oil and Products

—— Oil, 12" or larger

—— Products, 10" or larger

━━ Products, 6" to 9"

○ Refinery, 10,000 to 49,999 barrels per day

□ Refinery, 50,000 or more barrels per day

Natural Gas

—— Pipelines

● Storage areas

0   100
Scale in Miles

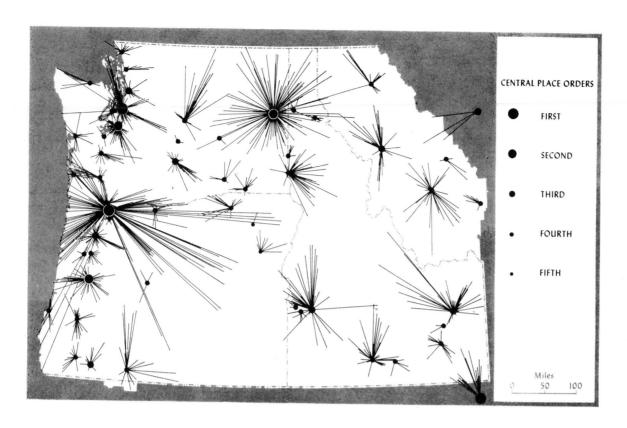

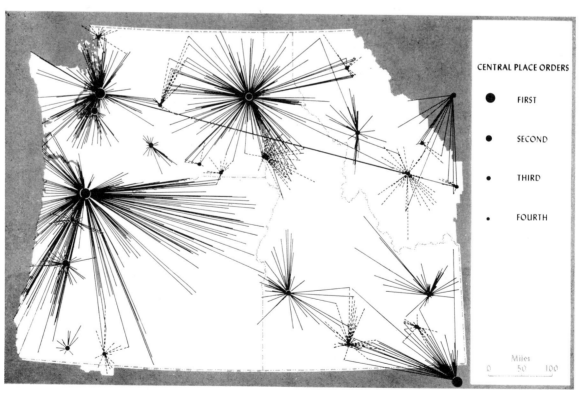

PRESTON'S NEWSPAPER CIRCULATIONS

PATTERNS of daily newspaper dominance in the Pacific Northwest (above) and of Sunday newspaper dominance (below) as depicted by Richard E. Preston in *Economic Geography*, Volume 47, Number 2, April 1971, pages 145 and 149.

THE NATURAL ENVIRONMENT
(above top) Cape Falcon on the Oregon Coast

(above middle) Mountains in the Okanogan National Forest, Washington

(right top) Cle Elum storage dam, Yakima Project, Washington

(right middle) Juniper country, Central Oregon

(right) Hells Canyon of the Snake River between Oregon and Idaho, deepest gorge in the United States

LANDFORM REGIONS

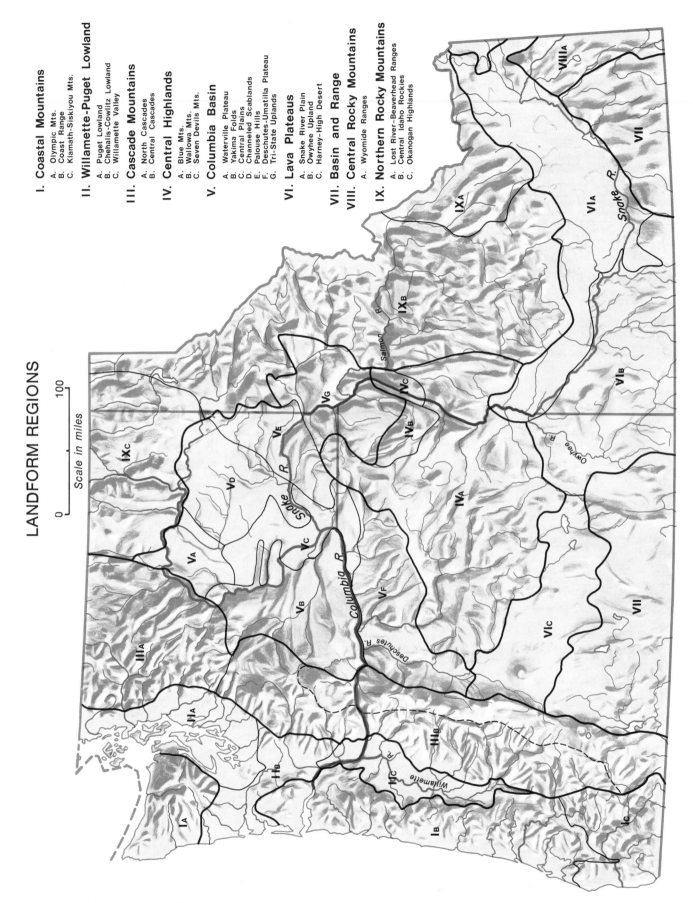

I. **Coastal Mountains**
   A. Olympic Mts.
   B. Coast Range
   C. Klamath-Siskiyou Mts.

II. **Willamette-Puget Lowland**
   A. Puget Lowland
   B. Chehalis-Cowlitz Lowland
   C. Willamette Valley

III. **Cascade Mountains**
   A. North Cascades
   B. Central Cascades

IV. **Central Highlands**
   A. Blue Mts.
   B. Wallowa Mts.
   C. Seven Devils Mts.

V. **Columbia Basin**
   A. Waterville Plateau
   B. Yakima Folds
   C. Central Plains
   D. Channeled Scablands
   E. Palouse Hills
   F. Deschutes-Umatilla Plateau
   G. Tri-State Uplands

VI. **Lava Plateaus**
   A. Snake River Plain
   B. Owyhee Upland
   C. Harney-High Desert

VII. **Basin and Range**

VIII. **Central Rocky Mountains**
   A. Wyomide Ranges

IX. **Northern Rocky Mountains**
   A. Lost River-Beaverhead Ranges
   B. Central Idaho Rockies
   C. Okanogan Highlands

Scale in miles

0   100

LANDFORMS of the Pacific Northwest range from rock-bound coastlines to snowcapped volcanoes and dissected lava plateaus. The major belts of mountains trend north-south, parallel to the coast, and provide indirect evidence of the pressures between the Pacific sea floor and the North American continent. However, much of the region's former landscape lies buried beneath great thicknesses of lava, in addition to layers of lake sediments and volcanic ash. Volcanic activity ended so recently that many of the cinder cones appear just as they were formed, and soil has not yet had time to develop on the newest lava flows.

Faulting is no longer active in most areas, although it helped create major mountain ranges, especially in southeastern Oregon and eastern Idaho. The extensive areas of hills and mountains owe their present form largely to stream erosion, and in some districts also to glacial abrasion. Of the major landform classes, true plains are the rarest in the Pacific Northwest, being limited to the Willamette-Puget Lowland.

The **Olympic Mountains** are the highest of the coastal mountain groups, with sharp ridges rising to almost 8,000 feet above sea level. The core was probably formed by the thrusting of old sea floor eastward under continental rocks; later stream and glacier erosion dissected the mass, and a few small glaciers exist at present. The **Coast Range** extends over 250 miles, and its consists mostly of low mountains with few ridges above 3,000 feet in elevation. Much of the range is made up of marine sediments, as well as basalt flows and other volcanics. These were folded and eroded by streams down to a fairly level surface before being uplifted; after 1,000 to 2,000 feet of upwarping, renewed fluvial downcutting created the present complex of ridges and valleys. The few peaks that stand above the general level, like Marys Peak and Saddle Mountain, are remnants of resistant basalt.

Geologically distinct and somewhat more rugged are the **Klamath-Siskiyou Mountains**, which have been sculptured from older, more resistant rocks. Summits increase in height inland, reaching an average of 4,000 feet in the Siskiyous, with the highest peaks above 7,000 feet. Steep-walled valleys contrast with gentler slopes above, as a result of changing rates of erosion.

The rolling to flat topography of the **Willamette-Puget Lowland** has developed largely by deposition in a structural depression. In the Puget Sound area, an ice lobe left moraine, outwash gravels, and glacial spillways. Later, the melting of glaciers caused a rise in sea level, creating a complex of channels and islands. Low rolling hills of the Chehalis-Cowlitz valleys have more exposures of bedrock, but glacial outwash terraces as well. The fairly level Willamette Valley is an alluvium-filled depression between the mountain uplifts to east and west. Terrace remnants of former floodplains occur at several different levels, and the central portion of the valley is interrupted by partially buried bedrock hills.

Chapman Point near Cannon Beach, Oregon, consists of intrusive basalt, in contrast to adjacent weaker rocks. Onion Peak is a remnant of lava flows which once covered the area.

Glacier-covered Mt. Hood dominates this view of the lower Willamette Valley, looking eastward near Wilsonville. Here the Willamette meanders between fifty-foot alluvial terraces.

The **Cascade Mountains** extend about 800 miles from British Columbia into northern California, with several subregions based upon topographic and structural differences. In the North Cascades, older rocks have been folded and metamorphosed, and were later intruded by small granitic masses. Glaciers as well as mountain torrents eroded steep-sided valleys over 2,000 feet deep, with the trough of Lake Chelan being an impressive example. Much of the area has summits between 6,000 and 8,000 feet, but two volcanic cones (Glacier Peak and Mt. Baker) rise higher. Numerous small glaciers blend in with snowcapped peaks.

In considerable contrast are the Central Cascades of Oregon and southern Washington, composed of volcanic rocks. Although this portion generally has less relief than the North Cascades, it has more numerous prominent peaks. The eastern, high Cascades of Oregon especially are dominated by a series of snowcapped volcanoes in various stages of dissection, standing on a lava plateau. Mt. Jefferson and Mt. Hood both rise above 10,000 feet, and in Washington, Mt. Rainier is a landmark for many miles, being the highest peak of the Cascades. The western Cascades in Oregon are a forty-mile-wide belt of older volcanics, much dissected and dipping gently westward. The Central Cascades as a whole owe their height not only to the outpouring of lava and pyroclastics, but also to uplift.

Between the Central Cascades and the Idaho Rockies lie the **Central Highlands**, a large dissected area formed by upwarping along a northeast-trending axis. Most of the region is referred to as the Blue Mountains (excluding the Wallowa and Seven Devils ranges). Basaltic hills dominate the margins, and there is a gradual rise from the plateau on the south; the north side drops more steeply toward the Columbia. Granite and older sedimentary rocks make up the peaks near the center, which reach 8,000 feet in elevation. Faulting controls some of the features in the eastern section, where there are a few structural basins like Baker Valley, filled with alluvium.

Farther east lie the rugged Wallowa and Seven Devils mountain complexes, separated by a dissected plateau and a giant gorge. The lava-covered Wallowas were uplifted by faulting, and much of the basaltic cover was later removed. In addition, three advances of ice widened and steepened the valleys. In contrast to the 9,000-foot crest of the Wallowas is Hells Canyon to the east, where the Snake River carved its way through the rising Blue Mountain uplift. The resulting canyon sinks over 7,000 feet below the highlands on either side, making it the deepest gorge in North America.

Rising abruptly on the east side of Hells Canyon are the Seven Devils Mountains, formed by faulting and sculptured by fluvial erosion. The lava-capped peaks reach to more than 9,000 feet and are separated by steep valleys, north-south fault scarps, and a transition to the intrusive rocks of the Idaho batholith. Although many areas of the Central Highlands have low to moderate relief, the major ranges and canyons have spectacular topography with more than 6,000 feet of local relief.

In the North Cascades, glacier-mantled Mt. Redoubt rises above a cirque containing Silver Lake. Farther southwest appear Mt. Shuksan and snowy Mt. Baker, thirty miles away.

Broken Top is an eroded summit of a shield volcano in the Central Cascades. More recent activity created the small cinder cone at right and the basalt flow in the foreground.

The **Columbia Basin** is here used to include most of the flatter, plateau-like portions of the Columbia River drainage basin, further unified by the presence of a Miocene basaltic cover. However, the lava is buried in many places by wind- and stream-deposited materials and also has been warped. A little-dissected area is the Waterville Plateau, the north half of which is covered by moraine from the Okanogan Lobe. At the northwestern edge of the lava floods lies the present course of the Columbia River. In south-central Washington, the basalt layers were folded into anticlinal ridges, with a general trend westnorthwest that is typical of this Yakima Folds subregion. In several places, the Yakima and Columbia rivers cut water gaps during uplift of the ridges. Some of the east-west ridges extend into the flat alluvial basin of the Central Plains, thus separating the Quincy from the Pasco basin.

The unusual combination of exposed lava uplands and a complex of former stream channels has given the name "Channeled Scablands" to a sizable area of eastern Washington. The channels or coulees were scoured by meltwater streams, possibly when glacial Lake Missoula emptied in catastrophic floods. Rock basins and scarps in the coulees are related to stream action and former waterfalls. Grand Coulee is an outstanding example of a former channel, created by the Columbia River at a time when it had been diverted by the ice of the Okanogan Lobe. To the east, there is a transition toward thicker deposits of wind-blown silt, or loess. This area of gently rolling loess-covered terrain is known as the Palouse Hills, and it extends eastward to the Rockies. The parallel ridges of the southwestern district are quite distinct from the more common dendritic pattern typical in the northeast.

More pronounced relief is found in the dissected plateaus of the southern and southeastern parts of the Columbia Basin. Extending over 100 miles between the Columbia River and the Blue Mountains, the Deschutes-Umatilla Plateau is crossed by several north-flowing rivers. These have eroded canyons from 1,000 to 2,000 feet deep in the northward-dipping upland, leaving broad flat areas between. Somewhat similar are the Tri-State Uplands, where the Clearwater and Snake rivers have incised steep gorges in a plateau.

Geographically separate from the Columbia Basin is the **Lava Plateaus** region, extending 500 miles from the Central Cascades eastward to Wyoming. Miocene basalts dominate as in the Columbia Basin, but there are also large expanses of Quaternary volcanics and some faulted landforms. The Snake River Plain is technically a plateau, with a gentle westward dip from 6,000 feet to 3,500 feet in elevation. One of the flattest parts of the Pacific Northwest, the plain is marked by scattered volcanic hills and some dissection along the Snake River. Both fissure eruptions and coalescing shield volcanoes filled in the broad structural trough, lying between the northern Rockies and the ranges to the south. Even the freshest-appearing flows are probably 500 years old, as measured in the groups of cinder cones called Craters of the Moon.

In eastern Washington, the barren and irregular surface of the Channeled Scablands in the distance contrasts with the soft contours of the loess-mantled Palouse Hills adjoining.

Lava flows of different ages are quite distinct on the 5,000-foot high Snake River Plain, west of Idaho Falls. To the northest looms the Lost River Range of the Rockies. (J. S. Shelton, *Geology Illustrated,* © W. H. Freeman and Co.)

The large central section of the Lava Plateaus is fairly irregular in topography, and is called the Owyhee Upland. Bounded on the west by fault systems and on the north and east by the Snake River Plain, the upland is an up-warped plateau with a basalt cover. The Owyhee and other north-flowing tributaries of the Snake River have dissected the margins of the highland region, with local relief increasing eastward from the fairly flat area on the western margin. The 7,000-foot peaks of the Owyhee Mountains are of granite, exposed by erosion after uplift between parallel faults.

The third portion of the Lava Plateaus is the Harney-High Desert area. Little dissected, this area has mainly internal drainage, although the Deschutes River crosses the western end. Newberry Crater is a caldera formed by steam explosions, and its flanks are dotted with small cinder cones. Much of the area farther east is quite flat, with low ridges trending northwest; playas and dunes of pumice sand are found in some of the basins. Occasional low mountains rise 1,000 feet or more above the plateau, which averages 4,500 feet above sea level.

To the south lies the **Basin and Range** region, dominated by north-south trending faultblock ranges and extending across much of Nevada and Utah as well. The portion in southern Oregon shares some properties with the Harney-High Desert district: basalt cover, internal drainage, and faulting. However, in the Basin and Range region the relief is much higher, and the tilted fault blocks dominate the landscape. Abert Rim and Steens Mountain are among the major ranges, and Warner Valley and Summer Lake basin are downfaulted troughs in which remnants of Pleistocene lakes remain. Some of the higher scarps rise 2,000 feet above the adjoining basins, and the highest in the area, Steens Mountain, presents a mile-high wall toward the east.

The portion of the Basin and Range region in southeastern Idaho has generally higher relief than that in Oregon, with pronounced north-south alignment of the ranges developed on older sedimentary rocks. Lake Bonneville sediments occupy some of the basins. Adjoining this area on the east is a section of the **Central Rockies** sometimes known as the Wyomide Ranges. Here, older sedimentaries have been folded and thrust eastward along low-angle faults, with one of the major thrust faults extending from Bear Lake northward to near Idaho Falls. Many of the higher ridges reach 9,000 feet in elevation, high above the alluvial basins.

The **Northern Rocky Mountains** region lies north of the Snake River Plain and northeast of the Columbia Basin. This maze of steep ridges and valleys is the largest area of rugged mountain terrain in the continental United States, although high peaks are not common. The Lost River-Beaverhead subregion is distinguished by its high relief and northwest-trending pattern of faulted ranges and basins. The southwest-facing fault scarps of the Lost River, Lemhi, and Beaverhead ranges reach 12,000 feet, having the highest peaks in Idaho. Structural valleys between the ranges lie a mile below, and have been partly filled; each is drained by two streams flowing in opposite directions.

The west-facing fault scarp of Abert Rim rises 2,000 feet above Lake Abert in the Basin and Range region. Farther east lie Warner Valley graben and Hart Mountain fault scarp.

The rugged Smoky and Boulder mountains near the headwaters of the Salmon River are typical of the central Idaho Rockies. Stream-eroded ridges and peaks rise above 10,000 ft.

The Rocky Mountains of central Idaho cover a much larger area, with somewhat less relief and little evidence of lineation. Stream erosion has thoroughly dissected the granitic mass of the Idaho batholith, as well as the faulted Precambrian rocks of northern Idaho. Although various districts are designated as the Clearwater, Salmon River, and Bitterroot mountains, there is generally no distinct separation between them. Some evidence of former erosional surfaces is seen in areas of fairly uniform summit levels, as in the Clearwater and Salmon River mountain groups. Typical of much of the Idaho Rockies are peaks between 7,000 and 9,000 feet in elevation, with steep-sided canyons 4,000 feet deep.

Between the North Cascades and the Pend Oreille Valley lie the Okanogan Highlands, a glaciated area of varied structure and moderate relief. North-south trending faults established the overall terrain pattern of alternating ridges and stream valleys. Glacial erosion also accentuated this pattern, as the Okanogan Lobe moved from the north. One of the most prominent ridges is the Selkirk Range, adjacent to the Purcell Trench and Pend Oreille Valley, marking the eastern limit of the subregion. Eroded along a fault zone, the wide Purcell Trench was also scoured by ice.

The coastal outline of the Pacific Northwest appears quite smooth, except for the Puget Sound area. One of the reasons for this is that the actions of waves and currents tend to wear away promontories and fill in bays. There are, however, numerous estuaries and headlands which interrupt the coastline. Estuaries form when a general rise in sea level drowns the lower portions of stream valleys. The complex of channels in Puget Sound, the wide mouth of the Columbia River, and Tillamook Bay all resulted from this process. Where resistant intrusive rocks appear on the shoreline, they wear back more slowly and thus form headlands like Cape Lookout or Cape Foulweather. Other common features of the coast are marine terraces, leveled by wave erosion when sea level was relatively higher than at present; and sand dunes, formed where weaker rocks supplied material for waves and wind.

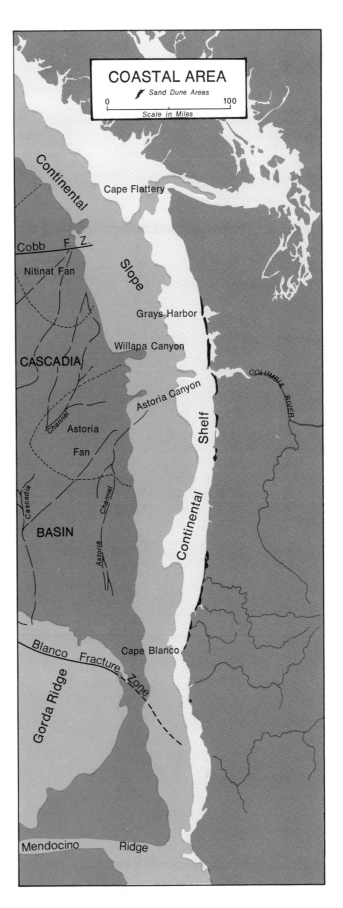

COASTAL AREA

Sand Dune Areas

0 ————————— 100

Scale in Miles

Continental Slope

Cape Flattery

Cobb F. Z.

Nitinat Fan

Grays Harbor

Willapa Canyon

CASCADIA

Astoria Canyon

Continental Shelf

COLUMBIA RIVER

Channel

Astoria Fan

Cascadia Channel

BASIN

Astoria Channel

Blanco Fracture Zone

Cape Blanco

Gorda Ridge

Mendocino Ridge

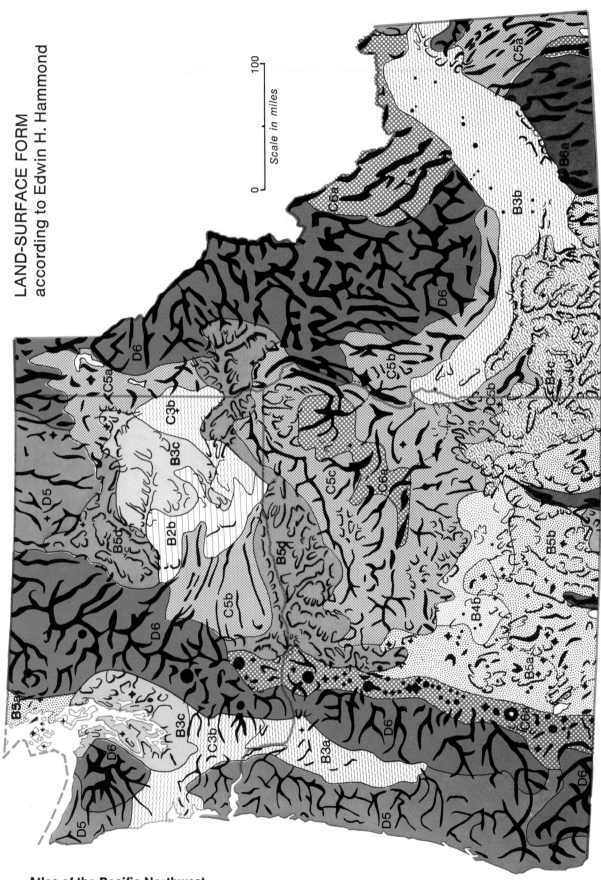

LAND-SURFACE FORM
according to Edwin H. Hammond

Scale in miles

0   100

Classes of Land-Surface Form According to Hammond

LEGEND

PLAINS

B2b	Irregular plains

PLAINS WITH HILLS OR MOUNTAINS

B3a,b	Plains with hills
B4b	Plains with high hills
B5a,b	Plains with low mountains
B6a	Plains with high mountains

OPEN HILLS AND MOUNTAINS

C3	Open hills
C5	Open low mountains
C6	Open high mountains

TABLELANDS

B3c	Tablelands, moderate relief
B4c	Tablelands, considerable relief
B5c,d	Tablelands, high relief

HILLS AND MOUNTAINS

D5	Low mountains
D6	High mountains

OTHER SYMBOLS

	Crests and summits
	Escarpments and valley sides

SCHEME OF CLASSIFICATION

SLOPE (1st letter)

A > 80% of area gently sloping
B 50-80% of area gently sloping
C 20-50% of area gently sloping
D < 20% of area gently sloping

LOCAL RELIEF (2nd letter)

1 0-100 feet
2 100-300 feet
3 300-500 feet
4 500-1000 feet
5 1000-3000 feet
6 3000-5000 feet

PROFILE TYPE (3rd letter)

a > 75% of gentle slope is in lowland
b 50-75% of gentle slope is in lowland
c 50-75% of gentle slope is on upland
d > 75% of gentle slope is on upland

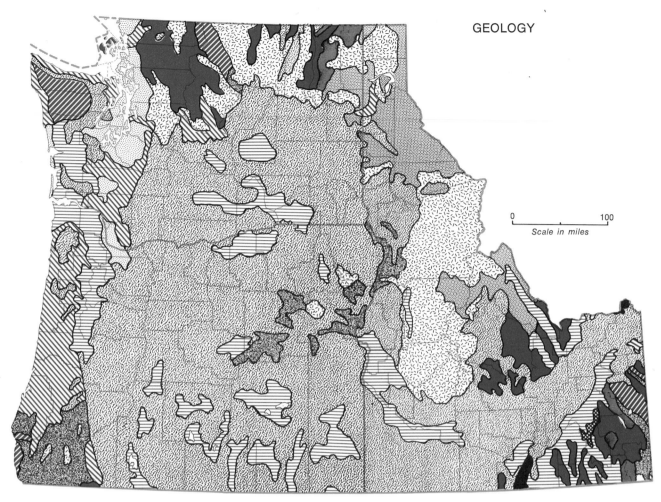

Scale in miles

0   100

Key to Geology

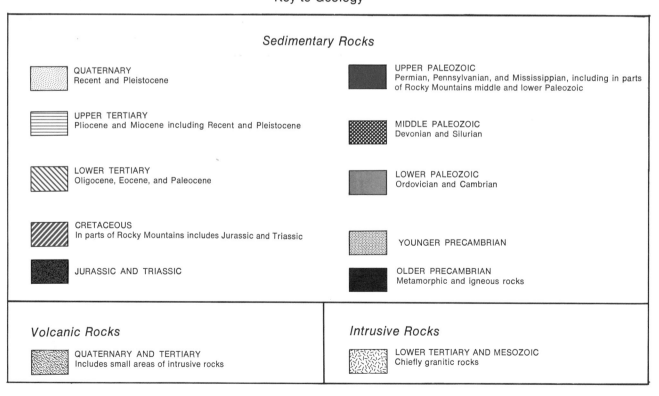

Sedimentary Rocks

QUATERNARY
Recent and Pleistocene

UPPER TERTIARY
Pliocene and Miocene including Recent and Pleistocene

LOWER TERTIARY
Oligocene, Eocene, and Paleocene

CRETACEOUS
In parts of Rocky Mountains includes Jurassic and Triassic

JURASSIC AND TRIASSIC

UPPER PALEOZOIC
Permian, Pennsylvanian, and Mississippian, including in parts
of Rocky Mountains middle and lower Paleozoic

MIDDLE PALEOZOIC
Devonian and Silurian

LOWER PALEOZOIC
Ordovician and Cambrian

YOUNGER PRECAMBRIAN

OLDER PRECAMBRIAN
Metamorphic and igneous rocks

Volcanic Rocks

QUATERNARY AND TERTIARY
Includes small areas of intrusive rocks

Intrusive Rocks

LOWER TERTIARY AND MESOZOIC
Chiefly granitic rocks

EXTREMES, as well as moderation, are hallmarks of the climates of the Pacific Northwest. These extremes are induced by mountains which shield an elevated interior from moderating, moistening winds from the Pacific Ocean. Sharp climatic gradients are also induced by these ranges; such gradients are exemplified by the mean (average) annual freeze-free period (Figure 1).

Above freezing temperatures persist from 240 to 300+ days from north to south along the coast but diminish to less than 30 days in the higher Cascades and mountains of Idaho. The Strait of Juan de Fuca, Columbia Gorge, Willamette Valley, and the valley of the Coquille River act as ducts through these ranges and allow milder air to flow into the interior, thus meliorating this organization in certain areas.

Not only temperatures but precipitation amounts and distribution are profoundly controlled by proximity of sea and mountains. The mean annual number of days with precipitation of one hundredth of an inch or more (Figure 2) again demonstrates a pronounced coastal bias, 180 to 210 days with precipitation occurring along most of the coast. Equivalent frequencies are found on the windward sides of the North Cascades and slightly lesser frequencies in the Central Cascades, Blue Mountains, and mountains of Idaho.

It is the Cascades, however, which create the major precipitation divide in the Pacific Northwest. To the west of the Cascades, with several topographically created exceptions, annual precipitation is always over 15 inches, while areas to the east, again excepting mountain zones, receive *less* than 15 inches of precipitation during most years (Figure 3). Frequent fogs (Figure 4) occur west of the Cascades with maxima along the coast, while to the east of the Cascades fogs are much less common. These climatic conditions control the varied character of agriculture and natural vegetation across the Pacific Northwest. However, seasonal variations in atmospheric flow create marked reorganizations of climates across the region.

Seasonal Windflow Maps

Preceding the seasonal climate maps are resultant seasonal windflow maps for the 850 mb level and the surface (Figure 5 for example). The 850 mb pressure surface is *approximately* 5,000 feet above mean sea level and the resultant winds for this pressure level suggest the net seasonal motion across the Pacific Northwest. This layer is intricately involved in the cloud and precipitation process. Atmospheric flow at 850 mb is chosen, then, to represent the basic current which carries appreciable amounts of moisture across the Pacific Northwest. Drier air aloft from the continental interior is also in evidence. *Surface* flows are so complex that no attempt is made to portray surface wind details; rather, the generalized resultant *surface* flow direction constructed by Mitchell for the mid-seasonal months of January, April, July, and October are entered for only the Pacific Northwest.

Note that on Figures 5, 12, 19, and 26, the area covered by the seasonal windflow maps is far larger than the Pacific Northwest; the purpose here is to indicate the general atmospheric flow in which the Pacific Northwest flow is imbedded. Glancing along the direction of motion of this general circulation one notes the flow turning sometimes leftward or cyclonically, sometimes rightward or anti-cyclonically. Resultant cyclonic flow in the lower atmosphere generally connotes relatively frequent storms, upward air motion, clouds, and precipitation, while lower atmospheric resultant anti-cyclonic flow suggests relatively infrequent storms, frequent high pressure cells, downward air motion, and diminished precipitation. On occasion, interesting variations to the general rules occur; one such will be discussed in this section. Details of seasonal flow will be delineated in introducing each of the four seasonal climatic discussions.

Wintertime Climates

With the exception of southeastern Idaho, the entire Pacific Northwest is covered by marine air in which cyclonic storms are imbedded. These storms and flow, however, are intercepted first by the Olympics and the Oregon Coast Range, then by the Cascades. Precipitation, largely in the form of rain (Figure 6), falls abundantly on lower southwestern and western slopes of these ranges with coastal mountains receiving the largest amounts. At higher elevations of the Cascades heavy snow falls. The total snowfall is frequently well in excess of 300 inches annually (Figure 7) and in certain areas, on occasion, this snowfall accumulation exceeds 1,000 inches annually.

In the rain and snow "shadow" to the east of the Cascades, with Pacific air flowing inland from the southwest, total snowfalls decrease abruptly. Annual amounts again increase on the southwestern flanks of the mountains of northeastern Oregon, southwestern Washington, southwestern and northern Idaho. Southeastern Idaho is under the domination of anticyclonic, subsiding flow and has much less precipitation.

As expected from the above description, the total numbers of hours of sunshine in midwinter (Figure 8) are restricted over most of the northwest. In the north, only the area to the east, or lee, of the higher Cascades of Washington, is sunnier. Southeastern Oregon and southern Idaho, to the lee of the higher northern Sierra Nevada Mountains and under the dominance of an interior high pressure cell, are much sunnier in winter.

The sheets of clouds which overspread much of the Pacific Northwest in winter serve to keep average maximum temperatures fairly uniform (Figure 9), with the elevated northern Cascades and mountains of Idaho the prime areas of lower midwinter mean maximum temperatures. Mean minimum temperatures (Figure 10) very clearly reflect topographic influences. The entire Pacific slope west of the Cascades, bathed by marine air, has mean minimum temperatures above 30° F with only the higher reaches of the Olympics and Cascades excepted.

This cloudy, moist, low level flow penetrates inland through the Columbia Gorge, keeping an appreciable area of southern Washington and northern Oregon less chilly at night. Only in the mountains of northeastern Oregon, southeastern Washington, and Idaho do mean minimum temperatures drop to values ranging from below 10° F to 0° F. Also pockets of nighttime radiational cooling are found just to the lee of the Cascades. These same patterns of minimum temperatures are reflected in the distribution of mean extreme seasonal minimum temperatures (i.e., the average *extreme* cold of the winter; Figure 11). It is noteworthy that the coastal mountains and Cascades do not show mean *extreme* seasonal minimum temperatures as low as those occurring in the mountains of eastern Oregon and Idaho or in the lowland areas just east of the Cascades.

1. FREEZE-FREE PERIOD
Mean annual number of days

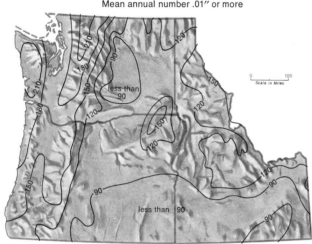

2. DAYS WITH PRECIPITATION
Mean annual number .01″ or more

0   100
Scale in Miles

Springtime Climates

As in winter, the springtime resultant 850 mb windflow (Figure 12) to the west of the Cascades is cyclonically curved, indicating a continued, though diminishing, frequency of storms traversing from west to east through the Pacific Northwest. After crossing the Cascades, this windflow curves anticyclonically over the plateaus of Oregon and southern Idaho, suggesting that the plateau surfaces below this level are heating with the advent of spring, hence readjusting the mass of the atmosphere upward to and through the 850 mb level. This condition ceases to be evident over northern Washington and Idaho, suggesting that surface heating may be less pronounced and/or cyclonic disturbances more frequent during spring.

With this spring windflow from above the Pacific Ocean being so similar to that of winter, the general geographic

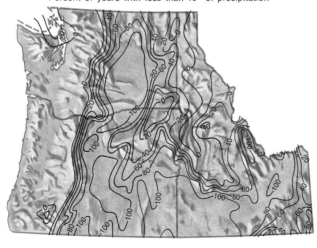

3. FREQUENCY OF DRY YEARS
Percent of years with less than 15″ of precipitation

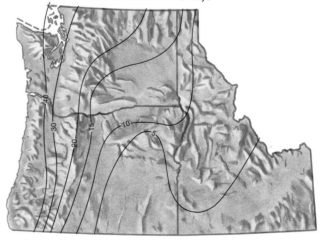

4. DAYS WITH DENSE FOG
Mean annual number of days

patterning of spring precipitation over the Pacific Northwest is also similar to that of winter (Figure 13). However, all coastal and mountain areas receive smaller seasonal precipitation totals, only 50 to 70% of the amount received during winter. Exceptions to this condition are the nonmountain plateau areas of Oregon and southern Idaho east of the Cascades. Here springtime precipitation totals increase slightly. This suggests that on occasion, increased surface heating to the east of the Cascades destabilizes the surface layer of air while cool marine air flows above. Strong convection and showers result. This effect is not evident in northern Washington and Idaho.

The increased radiant input reaching the surface on the plateau surface east of the Cascades is evident (Figure 15) with an excess of 260 total hours of sunshine during the average April. On the western slopes of the Cascades and coastal mountains the amount of sunshine decreases to less than 200 total hours; over the Olympics to less than 180 total hours during April. The mountains of eastern Idaho also show pronouncedly less sunshine (less than 220 total hours in April). This lesser amount of sunshine and higher elevations lead to lower mean maximum and mean minimum temperatures over the mountains of eastern Oregon, Idaho, and northeastern Washington (Figures 16 and 17). Also, more of the winter and early spring precipitation here falls as snow than on the lower flanks of the Cascades and coastal mountains.

This combination of circumstances leads to a much greater snow cover duration in spring in these northern and eastern mountains than in the west side watersheds of the southern Cascades and the coastal mountains where a larger percentage of the winter precipitation falls as rain (Figure 14). The net effect of these differences is to create a period of maximum flood threat to the Willamette River Valley in the winter, while the Columbia River Valley system, tapping a snow delayed maximum runoff from the mountains of eastern Oregon, Idaho, Washington and British Columbia, has a maximum flood threat period in late spring and early summer.

The distribution of April mean maximum temperatures (Figure 16) demonstrates, for the first time, the *cooling* effect of the Pacific Ocean. Now the coast, as well as the coastal mountains and Cascades, has lower maximum temperatures than either the Willamette Valley or the nonmountain plateau surfaces to the east of the Cascades. From the standpoint of mean minimum temperatures, all mountain areas show the lowest mean minimum temperatures, the coastal mountains below 40° F, the Cascades, Blue and Wallowa mountains below 30° F, and the mountains of east-central Idaho below 20° F (Figure 17). The plateau surface of south-central Oregon, separated from marine air inflow along the Columbia River duct by the mountains of east-central Oregon, has lower mean minimum temperatures than the plateau surface of central Washington, which is lower in elevation and continuous with the Columbia River source of moist, cloudy nighttime marine air. Such mean minimum temperature distributions lead to rather predictable variations in the mean dates of last killing frosts of spring (Figure 18).

Last killing frosts are before March 30 on the coast and lower Columbia River and before February 28 in extreme northwestern coastal Washington. In the middle and upper Columbia River Valley frost hazard ends, in the mean, by the end of April. In the higher Cascade areas frost hazard continues into June and in the mountains of eastern Idaho into July.

Summertime Climates

With the onset of summer, usually from late June to early July, the resultant 850 mb windfield undergoes a profound reorganization (Figure 19). Now the Pacific Northwest is divided into northern and southern flow sections, with the northern half still dominated by storm-created cyclonic flow from the Pacific. The southern half has cyclonic flow out over the Pacific, but within 100 miles of the coast this flow, while from the south, becomes pronouncedly anticyclonically curved. Over extreme southwestern Washington and most of Oregon an anticyclonic cell, with sinking airflow, is found. The 850 mb flow recurves cyclonically only in extreme southeastern Washington, eastern Oregon, and central Idaho, where the air, being closer to the earth surface and intensely heated, expands and recurves cyclonically. Still farther to the east this flow converges with an anticyclonic circulation from the south over the interior mountain states.

Sinking air in the high cell that dominates flow over most of southern Washington and Oregon is responsible for the dearth of precipitation over these areas during the summer months (Figure 20). An appreciable fraction of the precipitation that is received during summer falls from cyclonic disturbances during June. The areal distribution of this summer precipitation is noteworthy: largest amounts fall over the northern Cascades and Olympics, where the indicated cyclonic flow suggests a greater frequency of storms; very restricted amounts fall over the Coast Range and Cascades of Oregon with amounts diminishing progressively to the south. To the east of the Cascades, in Washington and Oregon, precipitation amounts are severely limited by the rainshadow effect of the Cascades and also by the strongly subsident anticyclonic flow at intermediate atmospheric levels. Only over the higher mountains to the east do slightly larger amounts of precipitation fall; this is usually associated with cyclonically related convective disturbances.

The same subsident flow at intermediate levels of the atmosphere, when combined with sluggish horizontal air movement and air-trapping effects of topography, leads to severe air pollution potential during the summer and on into the autumn (Figure 21). It will be noted that the southeastern Willamette Valley is particularly susceptible to this combination of meteorologic conditions: low level inversions and sluggish horizontal transport of air. These, with the advent of intense human use, lead to episodes of severe air pollution. The same natural conditions are extant to the east of the Cascades—in less densely populated eastern Oregon and the more populated areas of southern Idaho.

These aforementioned summer climatic characteristics plus increasing day length create increased hours of sunshine (Figure 22), resulting in high maximum and minimum temperatures (Figures 23, 24, and 25). Only northwestern Washington, particularly on the western side of the Olympics and Cascades, has a relatively small total number of hours of sunshine during July. While the same

(*Turn to page 54*)

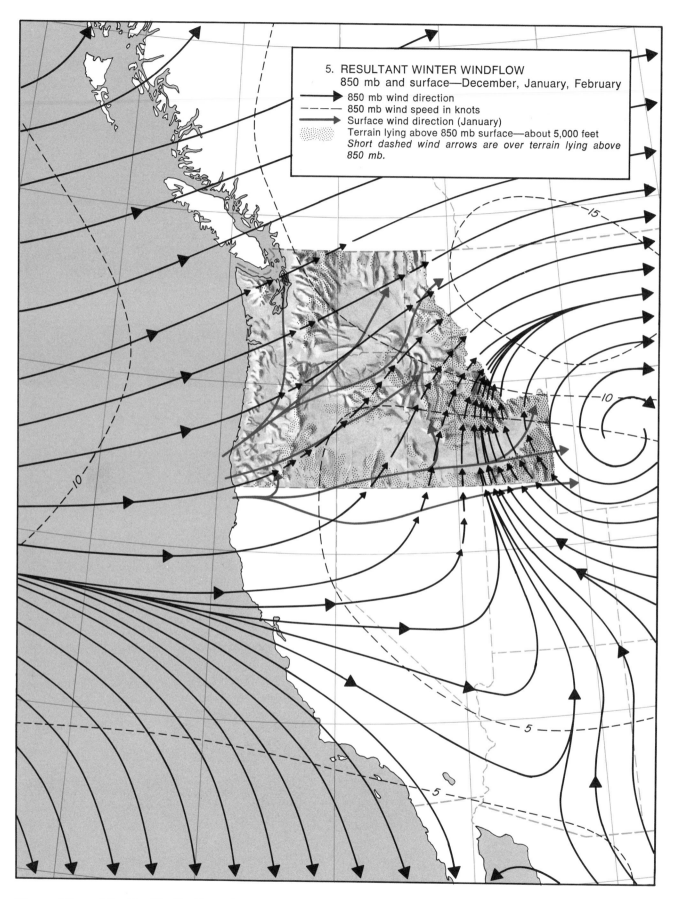

5. RESULTANT WINTER WINDFLOW
850 mb and surface—December, January, February

→ 850 mb wind direction
---- 850 mb wind speed in knots
→ Surface wind direction (January)
Terrain lying above 850 mb surface—about 5,000 feet
Short dashed wind arrows are over terrain lying above 850 mb.

6. WINTER PRECIPITATION
Mean number of inches—December, January, February

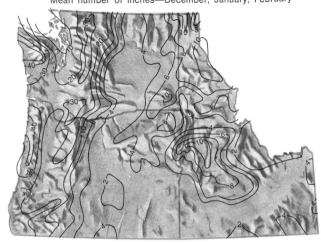

7. SNOWFALL
Mean annual inches

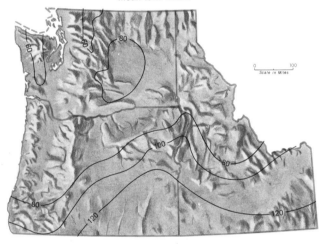

8. JANUARY SUNSHINE
Mean total hours

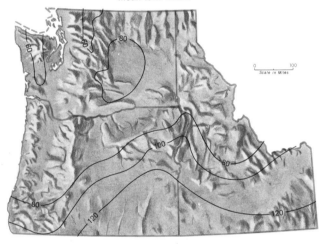

0   100
Scale in Miles

9. JANUARY MAXIMUM TEMPERATURE
Mean degrees Fahrenheit

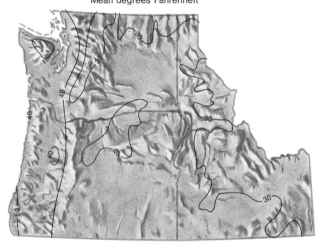

10. JANUARY MINIMUM TEMPERATURE
Mean degrees Fahrenheit

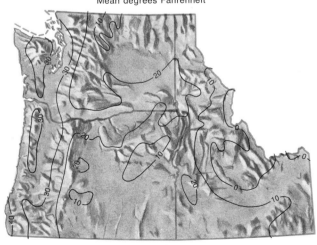

11. EXTREME MINIMUM TEMPERATURE
Mean annual degrees Fahrenheit

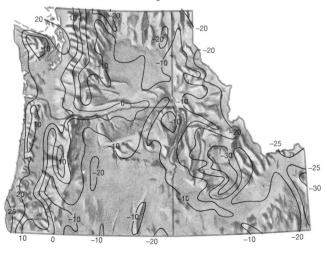

Climates   47

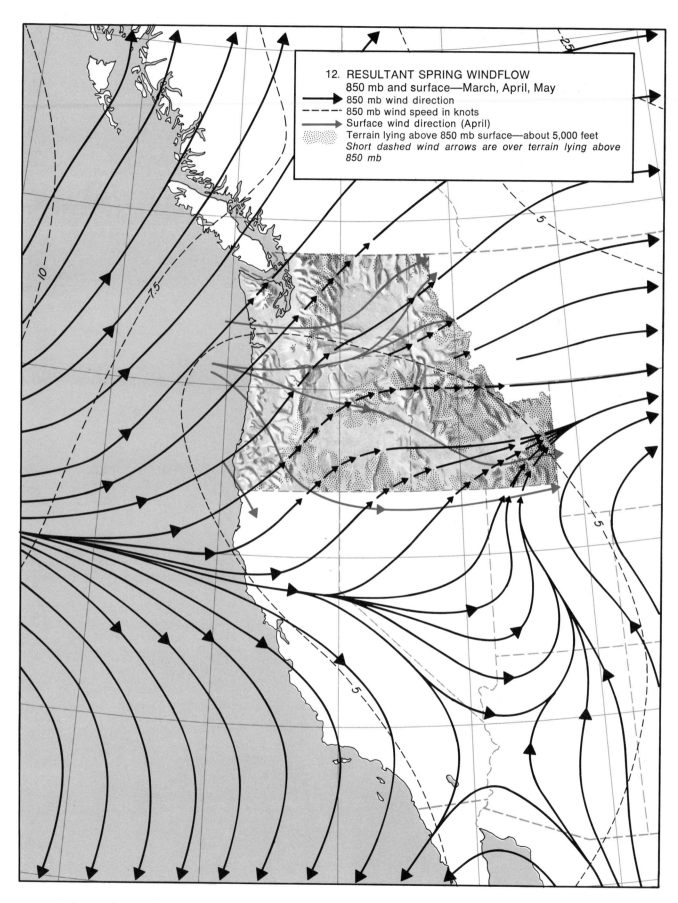

12. RESULTANT SPRING WINDFLOW
850 mb and surface—March, April, May

→ 850 mb wind direction
‑‑‑ 850 mb wind speed in knots
→ Surface wind direction (April)
⋯ Terrain lying above 850 mb surface—about 5,000 feet
Short dashed wind arrows are over terrain lying above 850 mb

13. SPRING PRECIPITATION
Mean number of inches—March, April, May

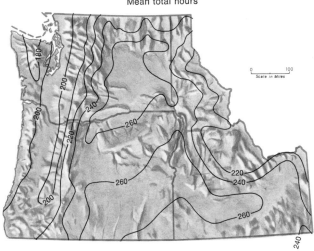

14. LATEST DATE WITH SNOW
Mean date with six inches or more snow depth

15. APRIL SUNSHINE
Mean total hours

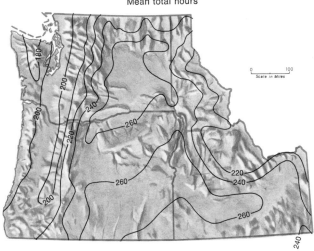

Scale in Miles
0 — 100

16. APRIL MAXIMUM TEMPERATURE
Mean degrees Fahrenheit

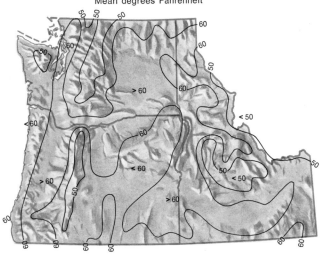

30

17. APRIL MINIMUM TEMPERATURE
Mean degrees Fahrenheit

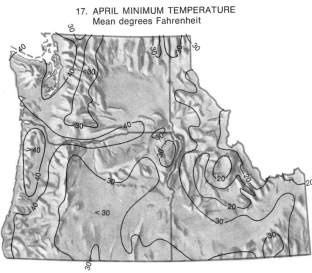

18. LAST KILLING FROST OF SPRING
Mean date

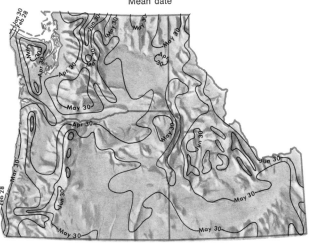

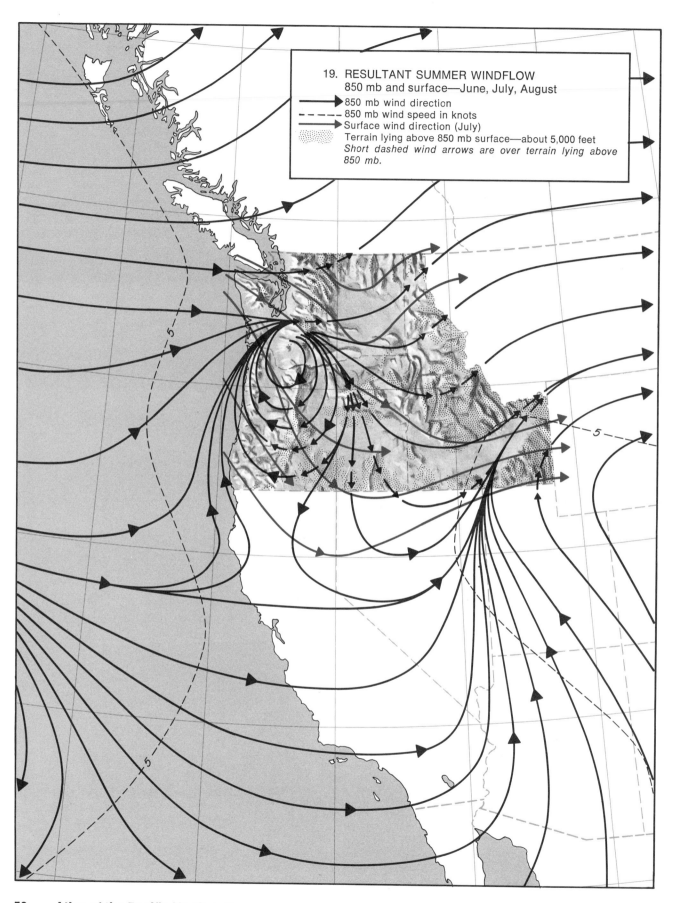

19. RESULTANT SUMMER WINDFLOW
850 mb and surface—June, July, August

→ 850 mb wind direction
- - - 850 mb wind speed in knots
→ Surface wind direction (July)
∴ Terrain lying above 850 mb surface—about 5,000 feet
Short dashed wind arrows are over terrain lying above 850 mb.

20. SUMMER PRECIPITATION
Mean number of inches—June, July, August

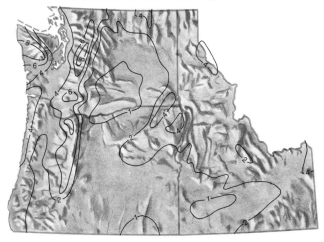

21. SUMMER FREQUENCY OF STAGNATION
Night-time windspeed 7 mph or less (percentage)
--- Inversion based 500 feet or less above ground

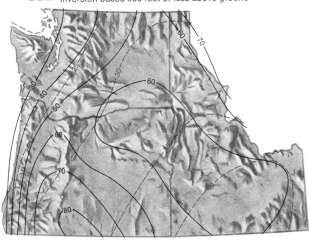

22. JULY SUNSHINE
Mean total hours

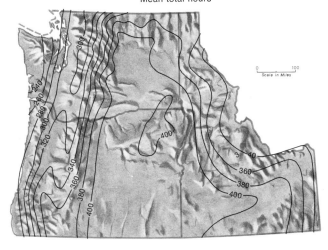

0   100
Scale in Miles

23. JULY MAXIMUM TEMPERATURE
Mean degrees Fahrenheit

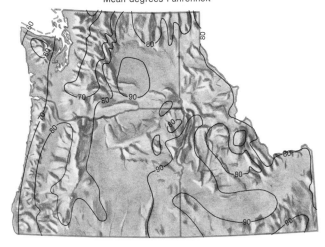

24. JULY MINIMUM TEMPERATURE
Mean degrees Fahrenheit

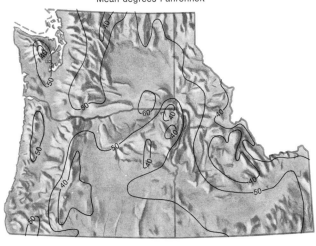

25. EXTREME MAXIMUM TEMPERATURE
Mean annual degrees Fahrenheit

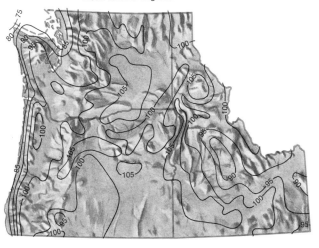

Climates 51

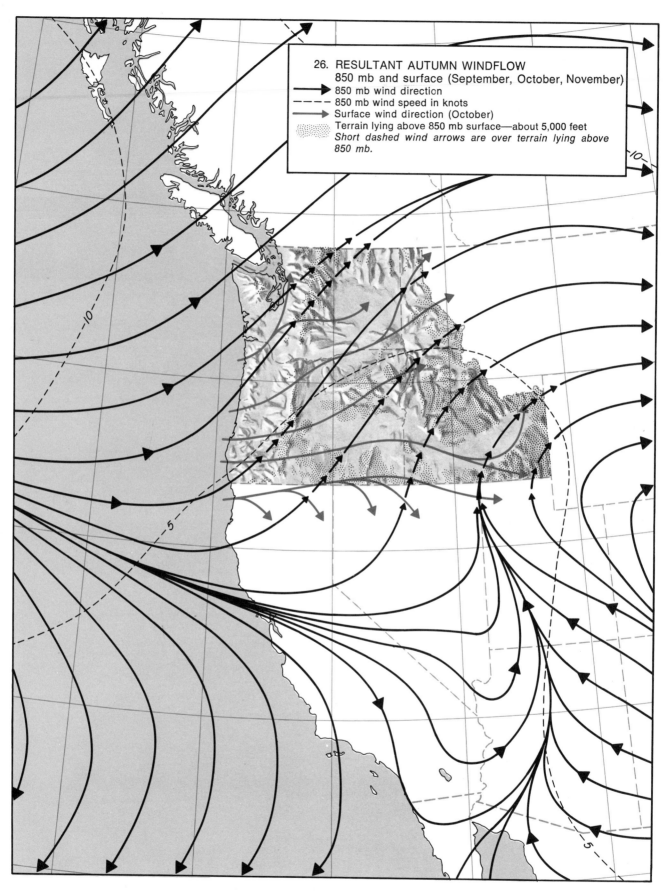

26. RESULTANT AUTUMN WINDFLOW
850 mb and surface (September, October, November)
→ 850 mb wind direction
‐‐‐ 850 mb wind speed in knots
→ Surface wind direction (October)
⋯ Terrain lying above 850 mb surface—about 5,000 feet
Short dashed wind arrows are over terrain lying above 850 mb.

27. AUTUMN PRECIPITATION
Mean number of inches—September, October, November

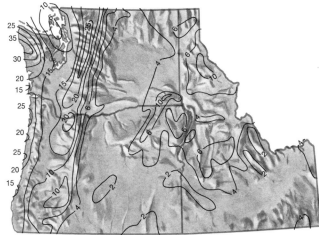

28. AUTUMN FREQUENCY OF STAGNATION
—— Night-time windspeed 7 mph or less (percentage)
– – – Inversion based 500 feet or less above ground

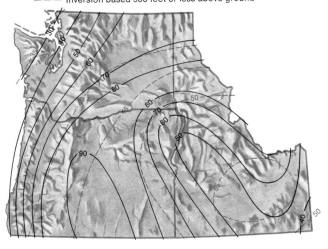

29. OCTOBER SUNSHINE
Mean total hours

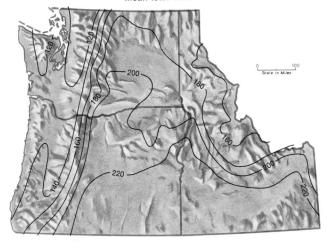

0   100
Scale in Miles

30. OCTOBER MAXIMUM TEMPERATURE
Mean degrees Fahrenheit

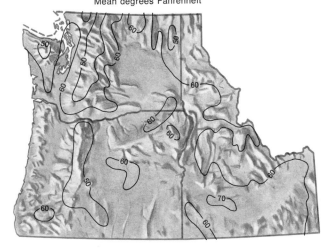

31. OCTOBER MINIMUM TEMPERATURE
Mean degrees Fahrenheit

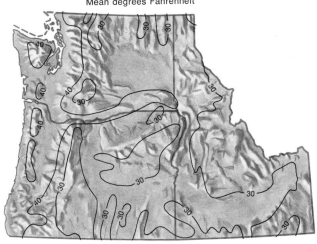

32. FIRST KILLING FROST IN FALL
Mean date

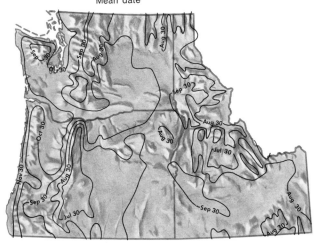

Climates   53

(*Continued from page 45*)

effect is seen in western Oregon, many more hours of sunshine occur during July. As before, the Cascades mark a major climatic sunshine "divide." To the east, most of the high plateau surface has more than 400 total hours of sunshine in July (12.9+ hours per day). Only the mountains of northeastern Oregon and eastern Idaho have slightly smaller totals.

Mean maximum July temperatures, with lower values west of the Cascades and high values to the east, reflect the amount and distribution of this increased summer sunshine (Figure 23). Even the higher mountains of northeastern Oregon and eastern Idaho have warmer mean maximum temperatures than do the coastal mountains. However, most summers bring spells of excessive heat (Figure 25) even to the coastal mountains, generally sparing only the immediate coastal fringe, where mean annual extreme maximum temperatures go to 75 to 80 degrees, while just inland, temperatures extend into the 90's and 100's. This situation is extent when extreme anticyclonic, sinking flow leads to heated, aridified air.

The patterns of minimum temperatures (Figure 24) again demonstrate the temperature differentiation created by highlands; the Cascades and the mountains of northeastern Oregon and eastern Idaho have July minima below 40° F, while the coastal mountains have somewhat higher minima. Lowlands and low plateau surfaces, particularly those connected to the Columbia River system, show higher minimum temperatures.

Autumn Climates

During autumn, the 850 mb resultant windflow so typical of winter and spring is reestablished (Figure 26). However, summertime flow patterns (Figure 19) continue to recur, albeit with diminishing frequencies through September and early October. The cooling autumn season provides an increase in cyclonic disturbances moving farther to the south across the Pacific Northwest, a situation made evident by the cyclonic curvature of the southwesterly resultant 850 mb flow across the Pacific Northwest. Only southeastern Idaho is within a continental flow during this season.

This marked change in atmospheric circulation from summer to autumn is accompanied by a pronounced reorganization of the magnitude and distribution of precipitation, sunshine or its lack, temperature, killing frost, and air pollution potential across the Pacific Northwest.

Autumn precipitation (Figure 27) shows a marked increase over summer totals on the windward slopes of the coastal mountains, Cascades, and the mountains of northeastern Oregon and Idaho. Especially pronounced increases occur on the southwestern slopes of the Olympics and the western slopes of the northern Cascades. On the northeastern, or lee side, of the Olympics a rainshadow effect is noted. Precipitation totals decrease markedly to the south along the western slopes of both the coastal mountains and the Cascades. To the east of the Cascades, precipitation totals, while markedly increased over those of summer, still remain small to modest. Only to the east, over the Blue and Wallowa mountains of northeastern Oregon and the Bitterroot and Salmon River ranges of Idaho,

do precipitation totals increase to values one-third to one-half of those noted in the Olympics and northern Cascades closer to the Pacific moisture source.

With this increased storm activity, clouds, and precipitation plus seasonal decreases in the duration of daylight hours, the total number of hours of sunshine diminishes rapidly. In October (Figure 29) the mean total hours of sunshine are approximately one-half those in July (Figure 22). Decreases are particularly notable on the western slopes of the Cascades and the mountains of Idaho. It is sunnier to the east of the coastal mountains and Cascades due to leeside openings in the clouds as storms cross these ranges. The interior high plateaus of Washington, Oregon, and Idaho, while much less sunny than during summer, still have almost twice as many sunny hours as the coast and western Cascade slopes.

The decreased solar radiation forces an appreciable drop in the mean maximum temperatures by October, with values now in a range from 50 to 60° F (Figure 30). Excepting the higher Olympics, the highest mean maximum temperatures are found in the coastal mountains, the Willamette Valley, and the interior high plateaus. The mountains of northeastern Oregon, Idaho, and northeastern Washington have lower mean maximum temperatures, with values between 50 and 60° F.

Mean minimum October temperatures (Figure 31) again demonstrate ducting of moist marine air eastward through the Columbia River Gorge, with nighttime averages remaining above 40° F. Everywhere west of the Cascades these same values obtain, with the exclusion of the coastal uplands. Mean minimum temperatures now drop below freezing in the higher Cascades and mountains of northeastern Oregon and Idaho. These areal temperature variations suggest when the first killing frosts of autumn may be expected (Figure 32) Along the coast, killing freezes are delayed until November, while in the mountains of Idaho they occur before the end of August. Areas that come under the influence of marine air flow through the Columbia River Gorge, as far inland as the Snake River Gorge and plain of southern Idaho, show mean killing frost dates during the month of October. As expected, the Cascades have killing freezes in September, a condition also extant across the southern Oregon high plateaus, where the drier atmosphere allows large nighttime radiant energy losses.

These same conditions lead to a fairly high frequency of nighttime inversions over these high plateaus from southern Oregon to southern Washington (Figure 28). Add to this, the propensity for wind stagnation in the same area, and all of the meteorologic ingredients for severe air pollution in the region are present. The southern Willamette Valley and Snake River Plain are only slightly less prone to the same condition. Fortunately, the large population centers of the Puget Sound lowland are less susceptible to this air pollution hazard.

Summary

The Pacific Northwest has many climates—some moderate and some extreme—with the ocean, mountains, plateaus, and large gorges all exerting pronounced control on the air circulations which specify these climatic variations.

Vegetation

Robert E. Frenkel

REFLECTING DIVERSITY in climate, soils, relief, fire history, biotic interaction, and historical development, the natural vegetation of the Pacific Northwest portrays a complex pattern. Although the pristine vegetation has been severely altered by human activity, the pattern depicted on the natural vegetation map shows vegetation as it might exist if the marks of man were eliminated, e.g., if agricultural, urban-industrial, and resource extraction activities are not shown. Major differences in vegetation, especially those determined by macroclimate, are displayed by fifteen vegetation types. Much more detailed maps employing more detailed classifications of vegetation are necessary to show local differences in plant communities related to soils, elevation, slope orientation, and historical development.

The system of vegetation classification and the naming of vegetation types employed here is based on the physiognomy (gross appearance) of the major dominants of the persistent vegetation under prevailing, normal, natural conditions. Thus, vegetation type units are roughly equivalent to climax formations (Küchler's potential natural vegetation or Daubenmire's zonal types) and define that general plant cover established on gently undulating terrain, mantled by deep, well-developed soils. Disturbance by animals (including man), by extreme climatic events, and by fire is assumed a special condition. The vegetation that actually exists will often reflect departures from the norm. Some of the major plant communities, variations, and gradations embraced within the broad vegetation types will be discussed in the expanded legend.

The vegetation of the Pacific Northwest is imperfectly known. A major review of the plant cover of Oregon and Washington has been undertaken by Franklin and Dyrness (1969). Daubenmire's detailed studies of the steppe vegetation of Washington (Daubenmire, 1970) and of the forest vegetation of eastern Washington and northern Idaho (Daubenmire and Daubenmire, 1968) and Cronquist, et al. (1972) review of the vegetation of the southeastern portion of the region are the major works which introduce the interested individual to more particular aspects.

VEGETATION TYPES (left) Douglas-fir forest typically found west of the Cascades crest, Ponderosa pine forest east of the Cascades crest, Western juniper and sagebrush in Deschutes valley, Oregon; (above) upper slope vegetation in the northern Cascades, Washington

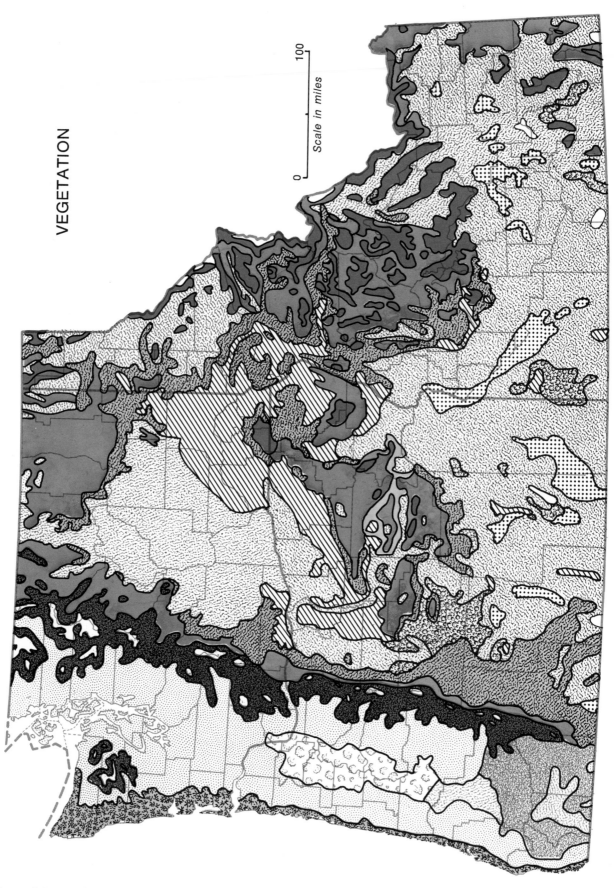

VEGETATION

Scale in miles

0　　　100

Major Vegetation Types

COASTAL SITKA SPRUCE TYPE: Confined generally within a few kilometers of the summer-cool winter-wet coastal strip, this coniferous type penetrates as much as 60-70 km up major valley bottoms in the Olympics, extends northward to Alaska, and grades into redwood forest in southwestern Oregon. Extensively altered by logging and fire, relatively few undisturbed stands remain. **Sitka spruce** (*Picea sitchensis*) characterizes the type although in many places **western hemlock** (*Tsuga heterophylla*) and **Douglas-fir** (*Pseudotsuga menziesii*) dominate forest stands. **Red alder** (*Alnus rubra*) often forms extensive patches in recently disturbed areas and riparian situations, while **western red cedar** (*Thuja plicata*) characterizes swampy situations. Beside coastal dune communities in which shore pine (*Pinus contorta*) is a prominent successional species, there are salt-marsh communities in estuaries and strand communities related to shifting dune systems along the extreme coastal strip. The Coastal Sitka Spruce Type rapidly grades into the Western Hemlock Type with which it bears close relationship.

WESTERN HEMLOCK TYPE: Mantling the Coast Range and the lower western slopes of the Cascades, this type is one of the most extensive in the PNW. It stretches north into British Columbia and south into California adjacent to the redwood belt and is especially important for timber production. Annual precipitation varies from 1,500 to 3,000 mm. Although named for the shade-tolerant western hemlock which characterizes the persistent vegetation, the dominant tree over much of the area is the seral species Douglas-fir. Extensive logging and agricultural clearing has occurred throughout the area. Other important coniferous species are western red cedar occurring in moist sites, **grand fir** (*Abies grandis*), and in the south, **sugar pine** (*Pinus lambertiana*), **ponderosa pine** (*Pinus ponderosa*), and **incense cedar** (*Libocedrus decurrens*). In disturbed moist sites, communities dominated by the red alder and **bigleaf maple** (*Acer macrophyllum*) are common. Plant communities within this type have been studied in considerable detail relating floristically defined units to site characteristics. Western hemlock gives way to Douglas-fir and, in some areas, to lodgepole pine on drier and sunnier sites; in wet situations as in northwestern Washington, western red cedar forms impressive stands; and as elevation increases and temperature decreases, **Pacific silver fir** (*Abies amabilis*) replaces western hemlock.

CASCADE SUBALPINE FOREST TYPE: An extremely complex series of vegetation types developing under heavy snow conditions is situated below the crest of the Cascades and Olympics and extends into British Columbia. Best regarded as a group of interfingering forested belts, this generalized type includes the Pacific silver fir zone dominated by *Abies amabilis* which commonly occurs above the Western Hemlock Type. At higher elevations, Pacific silver fir gives way to a more stunted, wind-firm forest dominated by **mountain hemlock** (*Tsuga mertensiana*) and **subalpine fir** (*Abies lasiocarpa*) both contributing to a park-like pattern of open meadow and forest stringers at timberline. In dry areas recently disturbed by fire or in areas of volcanic ash, **lodgepole pine** (*Pinus contorta*) prevails, typically forming even-aged stands. Species common in the Engelmann spruce forest of Idaho are frequently present in the northern Cascades. In southern Oregon the type bears close relationships to the red fir forest of California with species such as **white fir** (*Abies concolor*) and **Shasta red fir** (*Abies magnifica* var. *shastensis*), indicative of the affinity.

GRAND FIR/DOUGLAS-FIR TYPE: A mesic coniferous forest occurring in interior areas with some snow accumulation and exhibiting an exceedingly broad and complex distribution, this type embraces a variety of distinctive understory communities. Often both **grand fir** (*Abies grandis*) and **Douglas-fir** (*Pseudotsuga menziesii*) occur in mixed stands, although Douglas-fir tends to be more prevalent in Idaho and generally in warmer habitats. Other trees of importance in this type in order of increasing moisture tolerance are ponderosa pine, **western larch** (*Larix occidentalis*) and lodgepole pine; all of these species are fire-responsive pioneers. In moister, cooler areas in northern Idaho, western red cedar and western hemlock are prominent forest inclusions. **Oregon boxwood** (*Pachystima myrsinites*) and **common snowberry** (*Symphoricarpos albus*) dominate two prevalent understory communities.

PONDEROSA PINE TYPE: In a narrow fringing belt between the Grand Fir/Douglas-fir Type and Shrub/Steppe Type is a more open coniferous forest dominated by *Pinus ponderosa*. Understory vegetation varies from dense to open shrubby mats of **bitterbrush** (*Purshia tridentata*) and **snowbrush** (*Ceanothus velutinus*) in central Oregon to bunch grass meadows dominated by **Idaho fescue** (*Festuca idahoensis*) and **bluebunch wheatgrass** (*Agropyron spicatum*) further to the east. This type has been severely altered by timber harvest. Ponderosa pine, although persistent in this type, serves as a major seral species in the adjoining Grand Fir/Douglas-fir Type.

JUNIPER WOODLAND TYPE: In central Oregon this open woodland is the northern representative of the Pinyon-Juniper Zone, a vegetation type which is widespread in the Great Basin region and which penetrates the PNW region in southern Idaho. Shrub/Steppe vegetation dominated by **big sagebrush** (*Artemisia tridentata*) and by Idaho fescue typically comprises the understory of the Juniper Woodland Type. Commonly **western juniper** (*Juniperus occidentalis*) grows in open stands exhibiting a savanna type physiognomy. Throughout the arid regions of interior Oregon, juniper woodlands characterize rimrock habitats where local moisture supplies permit establishment of this xerophytic tree.

STEPPE TYPE: A distinctive plant cover of grassland without associated shrubs mantles large areas of north-central Oregon and the Palouse of southeastern Washington and adjacent Idaho. Since this grassland is very favorable for dryland farming much of the native vegetation has been severely altered by agricultural land use. Among the various broad communities identified within this grassland is the widespread *Agropyron-Festuca* type characterized respectively by bluebunch wheatgrass and Idaho fescue. In moister situations **Sandberg bluegrass** (*Poa secunda*) and Idaho fescue become more prominent along with a number of forbs and shrubby common snowberry. The Steppe Type has close relations to the more mesic ponderosa pine forest and more xeric shrub-steppe with the broad grassland communities commonly forming understory unions in these adjacent vegetation types.

SHRUB/STEPPE TYPE: Probably the most widespread vegetation type in the PNW, the Shrub/Steppe extends from the Canadian border in a narrow strip along the Okanogan River south into Nevada and west of the Cascades eastward to Wyoming and Colorado. Dominated by the aromatic big sagebrush, this type intermingles with the juniper woodland in central Oregon and juniper-pinyon pine woodland in southeastern Idaho. Stretches of this type have been transformed by irrigated agriculture in the Columbia River Basin; elsewhere the type largely supports nonintensive grazing. Plant communities within the type have been identified based on floristic composition of understory grasses, percent shrub cover, soils, and slope exposure. Two of the most prominent broad communities are *Artemisia tridentata/Festuca idahoensis* and the *Artemisia tridentata/Agropyron spicatum* types, the former having slightly greater moisture requirements. **Low sagebrush** (*Artemisia arbuscula*) frequently replaces big sagebrush in eastern Oregon in shallow stony soils. Commonly referred to as "desert," the Shrub/Steppe consists of nondesert species and exhibits a shrub-grass structure which is generally regarded as distinct from true deserts. Other shrubs include several species of sagebrush (*Artemisia* spp.) and **rabbit brush** (*Chrysothamnus* spp.).

DESERT SHRUB TYPE: Occupying isolated pockets within the broader cover of the Shrub/Steppe type, Desert Shrub is the most xeric plant cover of the PNW. Frequently the type occupies playas and playa margins where saline conditions characterized by salt crusts prevail, but the type also occupies the rainshadow areas on the lee of several north-south trending mountain ranges in southeastern Oregon and southern Idaho. Important shrubs, most of which are halophytic, include **shadscale** (*Atriplex confertifolia*), **salt sage** (*A. nuttallii*), **greasewood** (*Sarcobatus vermiculatus*) and **spring hopsage** (*Grayia spinosa*). Grasses and forbs are occasionally found in this well-spaced, low-shrub type. The type is best developed in the south and east of the region.

MIXED CONIFER/MIXED EVERGREEN TYPES: A highly complex type with close relation to several plant communities in California, this conifer and broadleaf evergreen forest is found in southwestern Oregon where it straddles the Siskiyou range. Edaphic, fire history, and climatic contrasts within this region lead to sharp breaks in plant cover. Douglas-fir dominates the upper canopy but various sclerophyllous evergreen trees are found in the low tree and shrub understory including **tanoak** (*Lithocarpus densiflorus*), **canyon liveoak** (*Quercus chrysolepis*), **Pacific madrone** (*Arbutus menziesii*) and **golden chinquapin** (*Castanopsis chrysophylla*). In more mesic situations, elements related to the Sierran Montane forest appear including Douglas-fir, sugar pine, ponderosa pine, and white fir. Areas of serpentine soil bearing a highly distinctive flora and depauperate vegetation are prominent in the Siskiyou Mountains. Other dry rocky areas in this range support a sclerophyllous broadleaf chaparral with **manzanita** (*Arctostaphylos* spp.) and *Ceanothus* spp.

ROGUE-UMPQUA FOREST-SHRUB TYPE: Occupying interior valleys in the rainshadow of the Siskiyou Mountains and southern Coast Range is a complicated mosaic of communities with many xeric characteristics. Woodlands are frequently dominated by **Oregon white oak** (*Quercus garryana*), with **California black oak** (*Q. kelloggii*) appearing on more mesic sites. Pacific madrone, ponderosa pine, sugar pine, and incense cedar appear in these woodlands and distinguish them from the woodland and forests of the Willamette Valley. On shallow soils and south slopes and in areas recently exposed to fire, sclerophyllous shrub communities are found with **narrow-leaved buckbrush** (*Ceanothus cuneatus*) and **white leaved manzanita** (*Arctostaphylos viscida*) as important species. Both the ponderosa pine forest and sclerophyllous shrub communities grade into related vegetation categories in adjacent northern California.

WILLAMETTE PRAIRIE-FOREST TYPE: Confined to the alluvial bottomland and adjacent slopes of the Willamette Valley is another complex mosaic of forest, woodland, open savanna with grassland understory, and prairie. Most of the original vegetation has been altered by agricultural and residential activities but also by changes in fire history. Apparently much of the Willamette Valley prairie and Oregon white oak savanna at the time of first settlement was maintained by aboriginal burning. Oak woodlands dominated by Oregon white oak often give way to invasion by Douglas-fir and grandfir with bigleaf maple becoming important on north-facing slopes. Grasslands presently maintained by grazing (formerly by fire) include a large complement of introduced species and tend to occupy drier sites. Lacing this mosaic of communities are narrow strips of riparian woodland in which **Oregon ash** (*Fraxinus latifolia*), **black poplar** (*Populus trichocarpa*), and species of **Willow** (*Salix* spp.) mark this special vegetation category.

WESTERN RED CEDAR/WESTERN HEMLOCK TYPE: Situated at moderate altitudes in relatively summer-moist locales in the northeastern portion of the region. this type is intermediate to the lower lying more xeric Grand Fir/Douglas-fir Type and the Spruce/Fir Type of higher elevations. Dominant trees include western red cedar, western hemlock, and **western white pine** (*Pinus monticola*), but grand fir and western larch are not uncommon in drier sites. Understory unions in the various identified communities in this type are similar to those of the Grand Fir/Douglas-fir Type with the exception of fern and Devil's club unions in moist habitats.

ENGELMANN SPRUCE/SUBALPINE FIR TYPE: Confined to the higher elevations of the eastern PNW region, this type is the counterpart of the Cascade subalpine forest. Varying from dense, moderately tall forest to open park-like stands, the dominant trees are **subalpine fir** (*Abies lasiocarpa*) and **Engelmann spruce** (*Picea engelmannii*) with occasional intrusions of **subalpine larch** (*Larix lyallii*) and whitebark pine (*Pinus albicaulis*) at higher elevations and in the north and Douglas-fir at lower elevations. Various communities within this type have been described and are differentiated mainly by understory shrub composition. In exposed situations near timberline the trees present krummholz form.

ALPINE TYPE: Found in true alpine environments near and above tree-line limits, this type is narrowly represented in the Cascades of Washington and Oregon and more extensively distributed in the Rocky Mountains. Although mainly comprised of herbaceous plants and low shrubs, there are a few trees displaying krummholz form and occupying habitats protected from excessive snow accumulation and wind exposure. Meadow communities found in the subalpine park area extend into the alpine type and commonly include species in the heather family (*Ericaceae*). Glaciers, permanent snow fields, and extensive areas of talus and rock cover much of the area within the Alpine Type.

Distribution of Selected Species

Distinct from the pattern of vegetation is the natural distribution or range of five selected prominent plants in the Pacific Northwest. These maps show the areas within which the species, including all varieties and ecotypes, may be found growing in a native or wild state exclusive of changes caused directly or indirectly by settlement. Outliers or isolated occurrences are shown by islands of shading. Many localities within the range of a given species will not be occupied by that species because of adverse environmental conditions; therefore, only the generalized distribution is shown.

PONDEROSA PINE
Pinus ponderosa Laws.

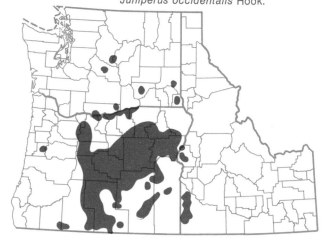

WESTERN HEMLOCK
Tsuga heterophylla (Raf.) Sarg.

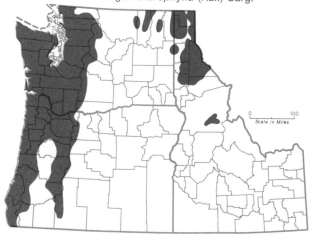

WESTERN JUNIPER
Juniperus occidentalis Hook.

0   100
Scale in Miles

DOUGLAS-FIR
Pseudotsuga menziesii (Mirb.) Franco

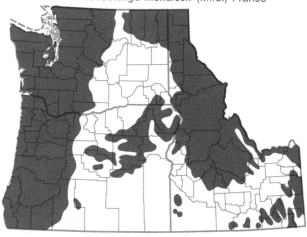

ENGELMANN SPRUCE
Picea engelmannii Parry

Soils ———————————————— Robert E. Frenkel

DIFFERENCES among soils reflect the interaction of several major soil-forming factors: (1) the parent material from which the soil developed, reflecting geology; (2) the climate which prevailed during the time of soil development; (3) the biota, especially the interaction between soil and vegetation; (4) the relief, reflecting the local physiography of the area; and (5) the time during which the soil developed.

Soils may be differentiated and classified in many ways; however, the major approaches in recent years have been by soil genesis or development and by soil properties. The classification system used here depends largely on soil properties and is the system adopted by the Soil Conservation Service of the USDA. The table below is included to facilitate comparison between the older genetic system and the more recent comprehensive system.

Seven soil orders comprising a total of twelve suborders are displayed. Soil *orders* are separated by generalization of common properties including horizon development and pattern, color, soil moisture, and degree of oxidation. In this way the differentiae selected for the orders tend to give a broad climatic grouping of soils. Of ten orders in this system, seven are present in the Pacific Northwest. Soil orders have the suffix "sol." The formative element of the order name is usually descriptive of soil, e.g., "Aridisols" are soils developing where there is little soil moisture.

Each order is subdivided into *suborders* primarily on the basis of characteristics which produce classes with the greatest genetic homogeneity. These characteristics include moisture regime, temperature, mineralogy, color, texture, and horizon characteristics. Altogether forty-seven suborders have been identified, twelve of which are shown on the map of the Pacific Northwest based on the dominant suborder. Suborder nomenclature employs a prefix for that characteristic which is important in defining the suborder and a suffix derived from the appropriate order name; e.g., "Argids" are soils in the Aridisol order with argillic or clay horizons.

Further classification of soils below the level of suborders involves *great groups* distinguished by the presence or absence of diagnostic horizons and other characteristics. The Soil Conservation Service recognizes 203 great groups and these are named by affixing a prefix of one or more formative elements to the suborder name. Therefore, a great group will be a three or more syllable term ending in the suborder name; e.g., "Durargid" for an indurate, clay-layered Aridisol.

There are also soil *subgroups* designated by two names, soil *families* differentiated on the basis of properties important for plant growth, and finally soil *series* each of which is a collection of soil individuals with essentially uniform differentiating characteristics. Soil series are given place names suggesting the fusion of the hierarchial soil taxonomy outlined above with real soils observed as soil individuals. Soil series are mapped and are described in considerable detail and provide the resource manager with important information. The *soil type* represents a lower category but is not included in the classification scheme. For a soil type, the series is broken down in terms of texture.

SOIL ORDERS IN NEW COMPREHENSIVE SYSTEM COMPARED WITH EXAMPLES OF GREAT SOIL GROUPS IN OLD GENETIC SYSTEM.

Order	Derivation of formative element	Examples of Great Soil Groups in old system
Entisols	Nonsense syllable, from "recent"	Azonal soils
Vertisols	L. *verto,* "turn"	Grumusols
Inceptisols	L. *inceptum,* "beginning"	Sol Brun Acide, Ando, Brown Forest, and Humic Gley soils
Aridisols	L. *aridus,* "dry"	Desert, Sierozem, Solonchak, Brown soils, and Reddish Brown soils
Mollisols	L. *mollis,* "soft"	Chernozem, Chestnut, Brunizem, and Brown Forest soils
Spodosols	Gk. *spodos,* "wood ash"	Podzols and Brown Podzolic soils
Alfisols	Nonsense syllable, from "pedalfer"	Gray-Brown Podzolic soils, Non-calcic Brown Soils and Planosols
Ultisols	L. *ultimus,* "last"	Red-Yellow Podzolic soils and Reddish-Brown Lateritic soils
Oxisols	F. *oxide,* "oxide"	Laterite soils and Latosols
Histosols	G. *histos,* "tissue"	Bog soils

SOURCE: *Soil Classification, A Comprehensive System* . . . Soil Conservation Service, 1960.

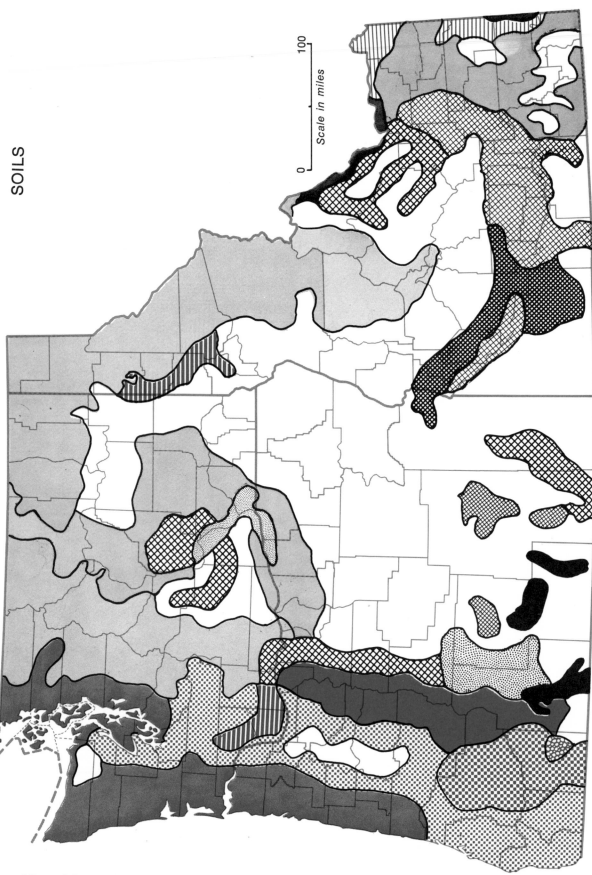

SOILS

Scale in miles

100

0

Soil Orders

INCEPTISOLS

Soils with weakly differentiated horizons exhibiting some alteration of the parent material and therefore soils initiating development. The B horizon typically has little clay accumulation. In the PNW, these soils generally occur under cool summer climate where parent materials are of a late or post-Pleistocene origin and do not show translocation of clay. The order is present in the Puget lowland, Coast Range, Cascades, and Idaho mountains. Two suborders are shown:

UMBREPTS are soils with surface horizons darkened by high contents of organic matter, having crystalline clay minerals, relatively high capacity to hold exchangeable cations, freely drained, and exhibiting acidic reaction. They develop in areas of high winter precipitation and moderate winter temperatures in the Coast Range, Oregon Cascades, and Puget lowland where western coniferous forest is the prevailing vegetation.

 Cryumbrepts—in cold regions.

 Haplumbrepts—in temperate to warm regions.

ANDEPTS are soils in the PNW with high contents of volcanic ash and are therefore of low bulk density. They are of recent development occurring in mountainous areas in Idaho and in the northern Cascades under cool summer conditions.

Cryandepts—in cold regions.

ULTISOLS

Strongly weathered and leached soils low in bases with clay-enriched horizons under moderately warm (mean annual temperature greater than 46° F) and moist (40 to 120 inches mean annual precipitation) climates, Ultisols develop in a variety of parent materials and usually exhibit considerable stability. This order is found in the low hilly regions of the Cascades and Coast Range where they generally support coniferous forest growth, display good drainage, increasing acidity with depth, and horizons with accumulations of silicate clays. Many are reddish. Two suborders are distinguished:

 Haplohumults—with subsurface horizon of clay and/or weatherable minerals; in temperate climates.

HUMULTS are highly organic Ultisols developing under moist conditions showing steep drainage and are mostly dark colored. They develop on steep slopes and are found in southwestern Oregon and the foothills of the Cascades and Coast Range.

XERULTS are freely drained Ultisols in areas of Mediterranean climate with little organic material in the upper horizons and are seldom saturated with water. They are confined to the hilly regions in the middle portion of the Rogue and Umpqua drainage and support a mixed coniferous-broadleafed evergreen vegetation with xeric elements.

 Haploxerults—with subsurface horizon of clay and/or weatherable minerals.

MOLLISOLS

Soils that have dark-colored, friable, organic-rich surface horizons, which are high in bases occurring in sub-humid and semiarid climates which may vary from warm to cold, are widespread in the region, especially in areas of steppe and shrub/steppe vegetation. These soils may have clay-enriched horizons, calcic horizons, sodium-rich horizons, or indurate horizons. Most soils are well drained, but wet soils may have soluble salts or high exchangeable sodium or both. Three suborders are shown:

AQUOLLS are Mollisols that are seasonally wet with a thick, nearly black surface horizon and gray subsurface horizons. In south-central Oregon in the Warner Valley and Klamath Lake area, horizons have been altered, but no accumulation of calcium or clay has taken place.

 Haplaquolls—with horizons in which materials have been altered or removed, but little calcium carbonate or gypsum.

XEROLLS are Mollisols in winter-moist, summer-dry climates. The soils are continually dry for long periods of time. With irrigation and when adequate natural soil moisture is available, these soils are important for grain and forage. These are the prevailing soils in the steppe and shrub/steppe areas of the region.

 Argixerolls—with subsurface clay horizon, either thin or brownish.

 Haploxerolls—with subsurface clay horizon high in bases, but with little clay, calcium carbonate, or gypsum.

BOROLLS are Mollisols of cool and cold regions. In the Pacific Northwest they are confined to the extreme eastern portion of Idaho.

 Argiborolls—with subsurface clay horizon, in cool regions.

ARIDISOLS

As suggested by the name, this order occurs in dry areas where the soils are never moist for periods of more than three consecutive months. The soils are low in organic content and the horizons are light in color and have a soft consistency when dry. These soils are found in the rainshadow area of the Cascades and in extensive areas in southern Idaho. Two suborders are shown:

ORTHIDS are Aridisols that display accumulations of calcium carbonate and other salts but do not have clay accumulations in horizons. Such soils are found in scattered localities in the drier areas of the Pacific Northwest.

 Calciorthids—with a horizon containing much calcium carbonate or gypsum.

 Camborthids—with horizons from which some materials have been removed or altered, but little calcium carbonate or gypsum.

ARGIDS are Aridisols distinguished by a horizon in which clay has accumulated. These are mostly found in Snake River Plain to the south of Boise.

 Haplargids—with loamy horizon of clay, with or without alkali (sodium) accumulation.

 Natrargids—with a horizon of clay and alkali (sodium) accumulation.

ENTISOLS

Soils in this order exhibit no horizon development. In the Pacific Northwest these soils are developing in sandy parent material and are of very recent origin on gently sloping terrain. They continue to receive parent material. They occur to the lee of the Cascade Range. One suborder is shown on the map:

PSAMMENTS are Entisols with loamy fine sand to coarser sand texture developing in areas of shifting to stabilized sand dunes. Sand origin is largely fluvial but with local redeposition by wind.

 Torripsamments—contain easily weatherable materials; never moist for three consecutive months.

 Xeropsamments—in climates with wet winters and dry summers; continually dry during long period in warm season.

ALFISOLS

Soils in this order are differentiated by clay-enriched horizons, moderate organic matter accumulation, gray to brown color, and are usually leached and are acid. Climate is cool and moist. Three areas are dominated by Alfisols—the hilly region north of Portland, the area northeast of Moscow, and the mountains near east boundary of Idaho. Two suborders are shown:

UDALFS are Alfisols with a mesic or warmer temperature regime and are almost always moist despite periods of summer dryness. These soils are brownish or reddish. The area north of Portland in which Udalfs prevail has a complex of other soils as well. The Udalf area in Idaho occurs in steep mountainous terrain.

 Hapludalfs—with subsurface clay horizon, either thin or brownish.

BORALFS are Alfisols of cool and cold regions and are rarely water-saturated. A bleached eluvial horizon often grades into a horizon containing clay or alkali. Found in mountains of eastern Idaho.

 Cryoboralfs—in cold regions; with sandy upper layers, grayish color, and subsurface clay horizon.

VERTISOLS

Relegated to this order are the clayey soils that have wide, deep cracks which form during the dry season. They occur in areas with marked dry-wet periods. One suborder is present.

XERERTS are Vertisols that have wide, deep cracks that open and close once a year, remaining open for periods of more than two months. In the Pacific Northwest, one area in the vicinity of Medford is characterized by this suborder.

 Chromoxererts—with a brownish surface horizon.

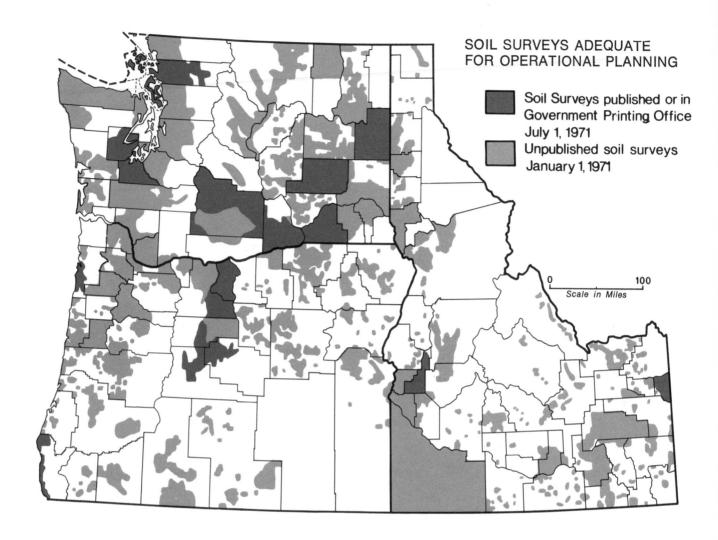

SOIL SURVEYS ADEQUATE
FOR OPERATIONAL PLANNING

■ Soil Surveys published or in
Government Printing Office
July 1, 1971

Unpublished soil surveys
January 1, 1971

0   100
Scale in Miles

Soil Survey Coverage

Depicted on the map above is the distribution of soil surveys adequate for operational planning as of January 1, 1971, in the Pacific Northwest. These surveys meet present-day requirements for modern soil surveys.

Soil surveys are made cooperatively by federal and state government personnel, usually with the Soil Conservation Service, USDA, in charge and the agricultural experiment stations attached to land-grant universities as chief contributors. Other agencies may enter cooperative agreements. Some of the agencies involved in soil mapping and soil studies either cooperatively or independently include the Bureau of Land Management, Bureau of Indian Affairs, Bureau of Reclamation (irrigability suitability studies), U. S. Forest Service, and various state forestry

departments. This joint effort, initiated in 1899, is referred to as the National Cooperative Soil Survey.

Most surveys are published cooperatively by the Soil Conservation Service and contributing agencies. Survey scale is usually 1:20,000 and the surveys are useful in conservation programs and land use planning. Advanced copies (before final publication) of soil surveys are available at local Soil Conservation Service field offices together with associated interpretive sheets. Published soil surveys, if still in print, may be purchased from the Superintendent of Documents, Government Printing Office, Washington, D. C. Surveys are available from the Soil Conservation Service to landowners or operators in the area and to other professional people as well. Copies are often available at other locations, e.g. county agents, Soil Conservation Service field offices, and libraries.

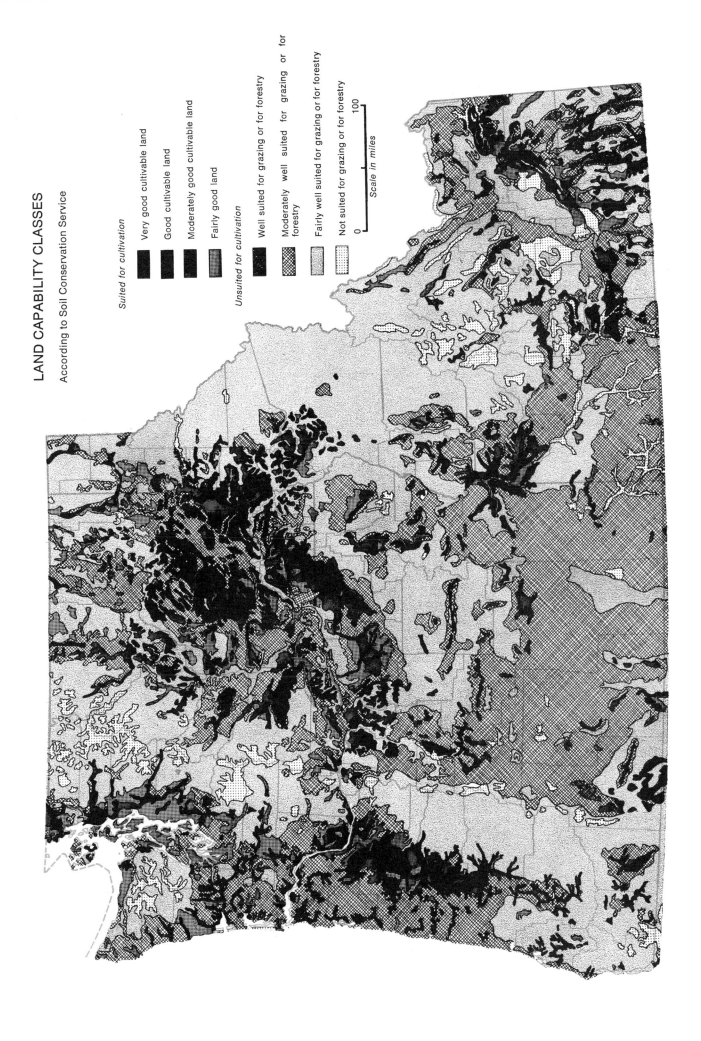

LAND CAPABILITY CLASSES

According to Soil Conservation Service

Suited for cultivation

Very good cultivable land

Good cultivable land

Moderately good cultivable land

Fairly good land

Unsuited for cultivation

Well suited for grazing or for forestry

Moderately well suited for grazing or for forestry

Fairly well suited for grazing or for forestry

Not suited for grazing or for forestry

0   100

Scale in miles

RESOURCES
(above) Harvest pattern in the Cascades
(right) Forest-to-mill log transport
(below) Cattle on the range

Streams in the high country collect run-off that is impounded behind dams and used for power production and irrigation.

Water ———————————————————————— Keith W. Muckleston

THE PACIFIC NORTHWEST is richly endowed with fresh water of relatively good quality.* The volume of runoff from the region exceeds that of any other water region in the conterminous United States, surpassing most regions many fold. In terms of per capita runoff, the relative position of the region is even more favorable. Temporal and spatial patterns of supply, however, vary markedly.

Supply

West of the Cascades the volume of runoff is unrivaled in the conterminous United States. In this western subregion rain-fed streams have maximum flows during the cool season. East of the Cascades much of the land is either subhumid or arid and traversed by rivers originating in various mountain ranges. Here maximum flows occur during the late spring and early summer. Over one-half of the Pacific Northwest (58%) is underlain with aquifer units that will yield moderate to large supplies of ground water. The potential value of these units is great as they generally coincide with populated areas.

The most significant source of fresh water is the Columbia River system. Rising in the Rocky Mountains of the United States and Canada, this system provides drainage for approximately 75% of the Pacific Northwest and accounts for approximately 55% of the total runoff. When runoff from Canada is included, the system discharges approximately 65% of the total runoff.

DISCHARGE OF SELECTED RIVERS

	Millions of acre-feet
Columbia River at mouth	180.1
Columbia River at The Dalles	133.7
Snake River at mouth	36.8
Willamette River at mouth	23.8
Skagit River at mouth	12.1
Rogue River at mouth	8.2

NOTES: Acre-feet are given to the nearest .1 maf. For the Columbia system, the average annual runoff is based on a 50-year period, 1897-1946 (water years). For the Rogue and Skagit rivers, regulated values are for base period 1929-1958 with estimated 1970 conditions of development. Sources: *Water Resources*, Appendix V, Volume 1, page 18, and Volume 2, page 782.

Use

Water uses may be divided into two major categories: (1) *flow uses* which utilize water within stream banks and

---

* Much of the data in this section refers to the Columbia-North Pacific Region used by the Pacific Northwest River Basins Commission (PNRBC). This includes the Columbia drainage in the U. S., coastal streams of Washington and Oregon, and the closed basin of south-central Oregon. Much of the material in this section was drawn from the multivolume framework study submitted by the PNRBC in 1970, especially *Water Resources*, Appendix V, Volume I, and *Flood Control*, Appendix VII.

◄ Grand Coulee Dam, June 1, 1971

include generation of hydroelectricity, navigation, fish and wildlife habitat, waste carriage, recreation, and esthetic appreciation; (2) *withdrawal uses* which divert water out of channel before use and comprise irrigation, public water supply (municipal and light industrial), and industrial, including cooling water for thermal electric generating plants. Excluding waste carriage, most of the withdrawal uses reduce both the quantity and quality of water considerably more than do the flow uses.

Water use in the Pacific Northwest is characterized by a heavy reliance on flow uses, especially for the generation of electric energy. In the latter half of the 1960s over 800 maf (million acre-feet) were used for this purpose yearly. This volume is much greater than the total runoff from the region because the same water is used repeatedly at successive power stations along several river systems. A relatively small proportion of the runoff is withdrawn for use. East of the Cascades irrigation accounts for approximately 95% of the withdrawals, while in the more heavily populated western portion of the region public water supply and self-supplied industry account for 70% of the withdrawals. Although much of the water from the latter two uses is returned to the rivers, a significant proportion of water withdrawn for irrigation is consumed. In the region irrigation accounts for 95% of the water consumed after withdrawal. A considerable volume (2.9 maf) of groundwater is used for irrigation on the Snake River Plain. Irrigation presently uses most of the groundwater in the region: 3.8 maf in 1970 as compared to approximately .5 maf by industry and .5 for public supply.

Problems

Competition between water-using groups has developed and will continue to increase. This is expected as an increasingly large population with rising per capita demands for water becomes ever more concentrated in urban centers. To the long-standing conflict between the generation of hydroelectricity and the preservation of anadromous fisheries, must be added the increasing incompatibility between leisure-time uses of water—often dependent on good water quality—and traditional uses of water. Problems of water quality are often the most pronounced near population centers where demands for leisure-time uses of water are the greatest. The planned construction of many large thermal electric plants over the next two decades will make the task of water resource management more difficult.

In the past, provision of storage was the usual response to water use problems. There are now more than 160 reservoirs with a capacity greater than 5,000 acre-feet; in 1970 approximately 42 maf of usable storage was available. But few suitable storage sites remain. Institutional measures will become a significant complement to existing storage. These measures include regulation of (1) water quality standards and/or discharges, (2) floodplain and related land uses, and (3) the siting of thermal electric plants and certain industries. A more realistic pricing policy and adjudication of water rights will also complement storage.

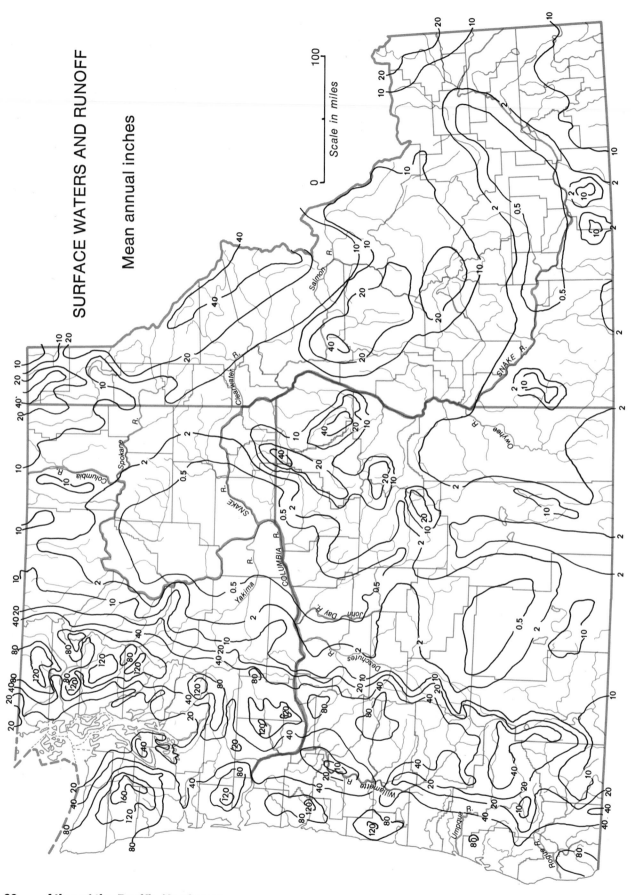

SURFACE WATERS AND RUNOFF

Mean annual inches

Scale in miles

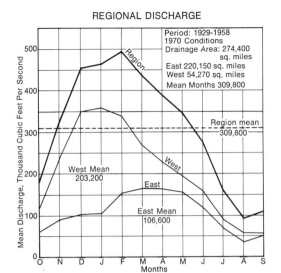

REGIONAL DISCHARGE

Period: 1929-1958
1970 Conditions
Drainage Area: 274,400 sq. miles
East 220,150 sq. miles
West 54,270 sq. miles
Mean Months 309,800

Region mean 309,800

West Mean 203,200

East Mean 106,600

Months

East - East of the Cascade Range
West - West of the Cascade Range

The graph (*left*) showing relative volumes of discharge from two subregions reflects the climatic dichotomy between the well watered west and the subhumid to arid east. The west, with less than one-fifth the area, generates almost two-thirds of the total runoff. (Note that this graph is not based on the calendar year as are the other graphs on this page). The three hydrographs illustrate the variability of yield and flow in the region. While the Columbia was selected because of its prominence, the Willamette and John Day are representative of west side and east side rivers, respectively. It is noteworthy that additional storage on the Willamette and Columbia has further modified their regimes.

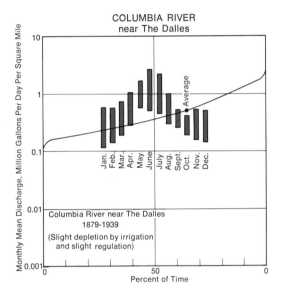

COLUMBIA RIVER
near The Dalles

Columbia River near The Dalles
1879-1939

(Slight depletion by irrigation and slight regulation)

Percent of Time

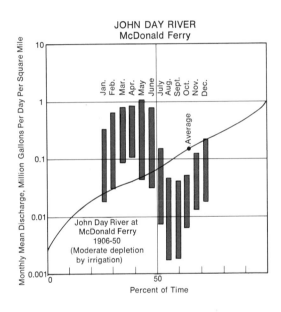

JOHN DAY RIVER
McDonald Ferry

John Day River at
McDonald Ferry
1906-50
(Moderate depletion by irrigation)

Percent of Time

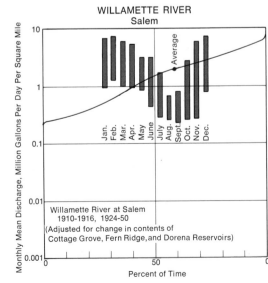

WILLAMETTE RIVER
Salem

Willamette River at Salem
1910-1916, 1924-50
(Adjusted for change in contents of
Cottage Grove, Fern Ridge, and Dorena Reservoirs)

Percent of Time

In terms of yield (mgd/sq. mile), the Willamette watershed exceeds the Columbia and John Day, 3.04 to .833 and .258, respectively.

The duration curves also depict variation of flow. The more nearly horizontal curves on the Columbia and Willamette graphs illustrate moderate variation, whereas the curve on the John Day graph indicates extreme variation. A sharp downward sweep of the curve at the left indicates very small flows are not uncommon, while a sharp upward sweep reflects relatively large flood flows at irregular intervals. Midpoints on the bars approximate average monthly discharge, while the length of the bar shows variation for each month. The Willamette is illustrative of a winter maximum-summer minimum regime, as contrasted to the other two rivers. The John Day has the greatest variation in each month.

Water 69

The map (*below*) of rural, municipal, and industrial water uses reflects population distribution, urbanization, and industrial output. Most of the municipal and industrial water use is west of the Cascades. Pulp and paper mills require about 60% of the total industrial withdrawals. Subregion 8 illustrates the significance of pulp and paper manufacture there. Food processing is usually the most significant industrial use east of the Cascades, but primary metals are significant in subregions 1 and 7. Although rural systems supply less than 25% of the total population, in two-thirds of the subregions they supply over 30%. In subregions 3 and 12 about one-half of the people are served by rural systems. Cooling water for thermal electric plants is not included. Within the decade, however, this category will become increasingly significant.

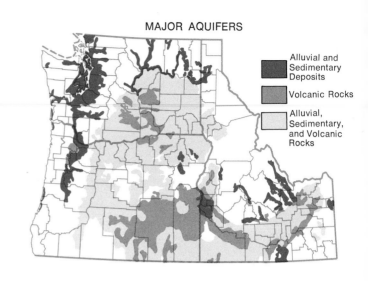

MAJOR AQUIFERS

Alluvial and
Sedimentary
Deposits

Volcanic Rocks

Alluvial,
Sedimentary,
and Volcanic
Rocks

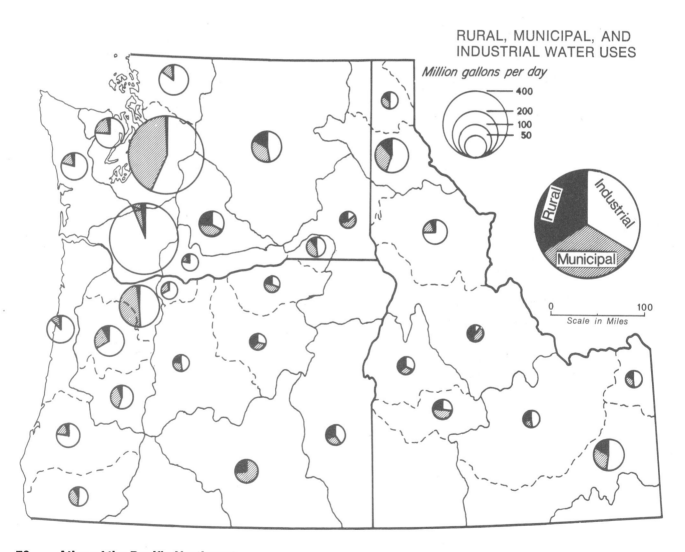

RURAL, MUNICIPAL, AND
INDUSTRIAL WATER USES

Million gallons per day

400
200
100
50

Rural
Industrial
Municipal

0   100
Scale in Miles

ELECTRIC GENERATING FACILITIES

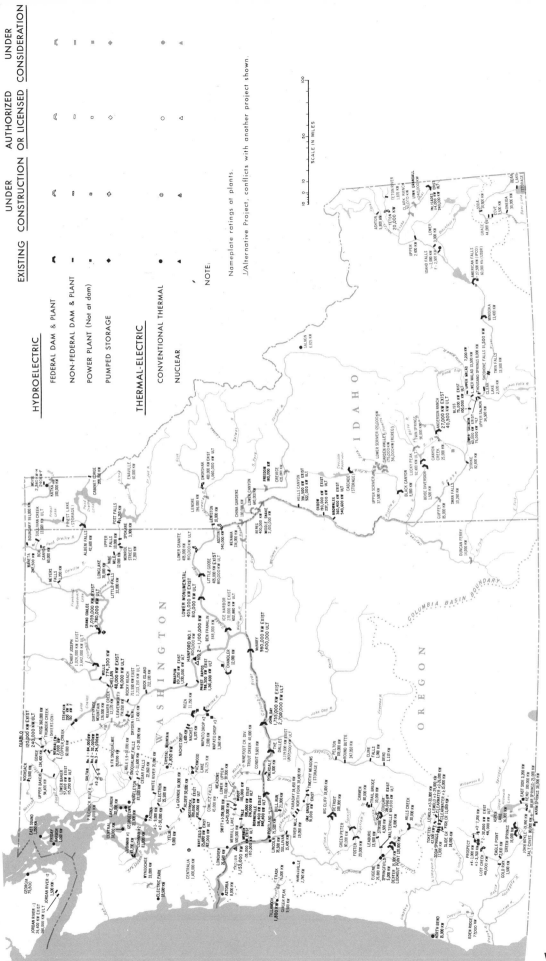

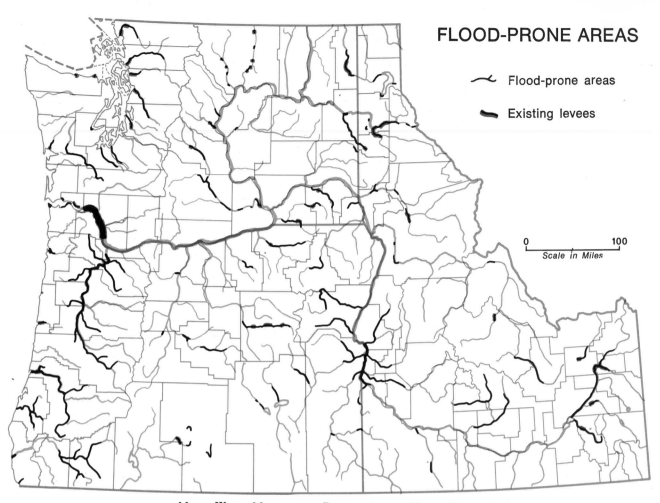

FLOOD-PRONE AREAS

⌐ Flood-prone areas

▬ Existing levees

0 ——— 100
Scale in Miles

MAJOR WATER MANAGEMENT PROBLEMS IN THE UNITED STATES

	Adequacy of annual natural runoff	Ground-water storage depletion	Water Quality				Flood damages	Water-shed lands	Beach, shore and riverbank erosion	Wet-lands
			Wastes	Heat	Salinity	Sediment				
North Atlantic	○○	○○	●●	●●	○	○○	○○	○○	●	●
South Atlantic-Gulf	○	○○	●	○○	○	●	●	●	●●	●●
Great Lakes	○○	○	●●	●●	○	○○	●	○	○○	○○
Ohio	○○	○	●	●	○	○○	●	○○	○	○
Tennessee	○	○	○○	○○	○	○○	○○	○○	○	○
Upper Mississippi	○○	○	●	●	○	○○	●	○○	●	●
Lower Mississippi	○	○	○○	●	○	●●	●	●	●	●
Souris-Red-Rainy	●	○	○○	○	○	○	●	○	○○	●
Missouri	●	●●	○○	○○	○○	●	●	●	●	●
Arkansas-White-Red	●	●●	○○	○	●	●●	●	●	●	●
Texas-Gulf	●	●●	●	○○	●	●	○○	●	●	●
Rio Grande	●●	●●	●	○	●●	●●	○○	●	○○	●
Upper Colorado	●●	○	○○	○	●●	●	○	○○	○	○
Lower Colorado	●●	●●	○	○	●●	●●	○○	○	○	○
Great Basin	●●	○○	●	○	○○	○○	○	○○	○	○○
Columbia-North Pacific	○○	○○	○○	●	○	○	●	○○	○○	●
California	●	●	●	○○	●	○○	●	●	●	○○
Alaska	○	○	○○	○	○	○	○○	●	●	○○
Hawaii	○	○○	○○	○	○	○	○○	○○	●	○○
Puerto Rico	○	○	○○	○	○	●	○	●	○○	○

●● Severe problems in some areas or major problems in many areas

● Major problem in some areas or moderate problem in many areas

○○ Moderate problem in some areas or minor problem in many areas

○ Minor problem in some areas

The chart on U. S. water management problems indicates that the Pacific Northwest is relatively well off. Heat is classed as a major problem in the region due to the low tolerance of anadromous fish to thermal pollution. Flood damage is another major problem. Despite the provision of considerable flood storage, levees, and channel improvements, many riverine lands remain susceptible to inundation. Lack of land control to complement the structural approach has allowed continuing encroachment into the floodplains. Flood damage does not vary in direct proportion with population. For example in the populous subregion 9, extensive storage has reduced damage appreciably relative to the less populous subregion 10 where most streams remain uncontrolled. Although flood damage to urban areas on major streams is widely publicized, rural areas along minor streams suffer greater losses.

KEY TO SUB-BASINS

SUMMARY, LOCAL PROTECTION PROJECTS, 1970 COLUMBIA-NORTH PACIFIC REGION

Subregion	Levees	Channel Improvement and stabilization	Bank protection
	Miles	Miles	Miles
1	161	1,168	488
2	20	203	205
3	64	128	......
4	171	119	131
5	48	192	1,042
6	29	436	407
7	72	366	106
8	449	100	176
9	......	368	115
10	202	383	129
11	578	......	203
12	......	......	20
TOTAL	1,794	3,463	3,022

FLOOD CONTROL STORAGE, 1970, COLUMBIA-NORTH PACIFIC REGION°
Storage in 1,000 Acre-feet

Subregion	Allocated primary	Flood control joint use	Incidental Major res.	Incidental Farm pond and small res.	Totals	Usable for control of Columbia River floods
Canada						20,900
1		10,319	335	24.0	10,678	10,552
2		5,232	24	21.0	5,276	5,232
3		......	1,071	4.5	1,075	......
4	10	1,716	3,108	51.0	4,883	1,600
5	97	2,270	2,120	97.0	4,584	2,783
6	....	2,000	......	11.0	2,011	2,000
7	8	577	471	38.9	1,094	500
8	100	260	1,850	3.3	2,213	......
9	....	1,703	......	17.7	1,720	......
10	....	65	......	9.7	74	
11	106	226	1,719	7.0	2,058	......
12				155.3	155	
Total	321	24,368	10,698	440.8	35,821	43,567

° Includes projects under construction.

REMAINING FLOOD PROBLEMS, COLUMBIA-NORTH PACIFIC REGION

Sub-region	1,000 acres Areas flooded (a) Major streams	Minor streams	Total	Average annual damages $1,000 Major streams Rural	Urban	Total	Minor streams Rural	Urban	Total	Bank erosion Rural	Urban	Total	Total
1	129	186	315	531	574	1,105	1,466	118	1,584	334	0	334	3,023
2	32	115	147	265	1,424	1,689	2,403	180	2,583	282	0	282	4,554
3	39	86	125	442	274	716	905	145	1,050	52	0	52	1,818
4	204	380	584	756	319	1,075	5,783	975	6,758	766	44	810	8,643
5	70	125	195	518	224	742	1,738	193	1,931	1,045	55	1,100	3,773
6	64	178	242	436	509	945	3,489	158	3,647	696	44	740	5,332
7	42	123	165	748	319	1,067	2,322	170	2,492	1,068	76	1,144	4,703
8	106	100	206	1,233	164	1,397	1,402	351	1,753	456	153	609	3,759
9 (b)	513	177	690	553	2,581	3,134	808	292	1,100	1,039	127	1,166	5,400
10	140	297	437	3,051	3,894	6,945	2,442	840	3,282	834	208	1,042	11,269
11 (c)	278	357	635	2,960	3,832	7,122ᵈ	7,833	989	8,822	115	0	115	16,059
12		184	184	406	262	668	785	16	801	0	0	0	1,469
TOTAL	1,617	2,308	3,925	11,899	14,376	26,605ᵈ	31,376	4,427	35,803	6,687	707	7,394	69,802

NOTES:
Table is based on 1967 prices and economic development, except as noted, and on 1970 structural protection including projects under construction.
(a) Plus scattered small areas.
(b) Data from Willamette Basin Comprehensive Report (2), 1965 price levels.
(c) Data from PSAW (1), 1966 price levels.
(d) Includes $330,000 not segregated between urban and rural.

WATER MANAGEMENT TECHNIQUES
Columbia-North Pacific

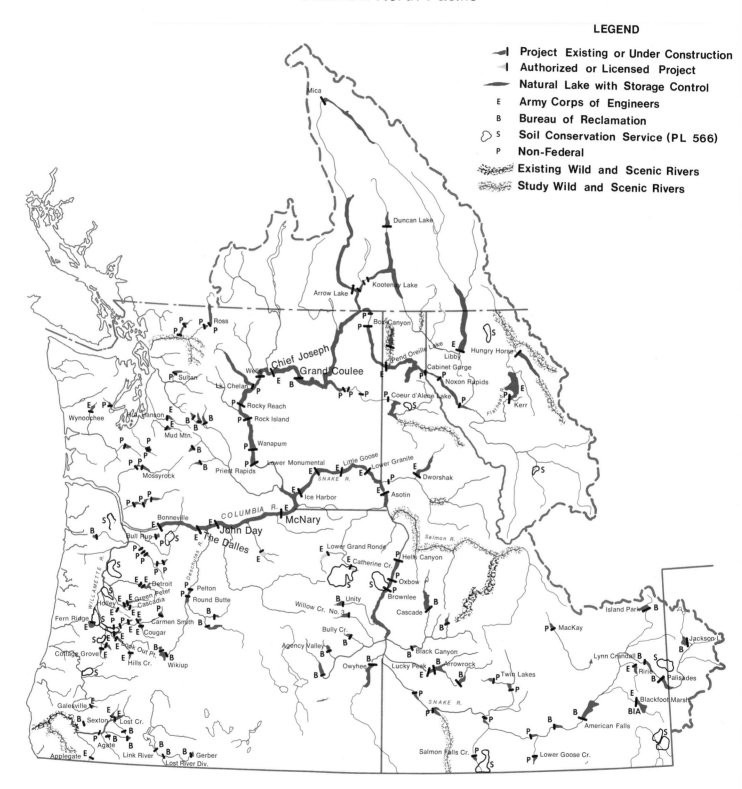

LEGEND

◄▎ Project Existing or Under Construction
◄▎ Authorized or Licensed Project
▬ Natural Lake with Storage Control
E Army Corps of Engineers
B Bureau of Reclamation
S Soil Conservation Service (PL 566)
P Non-Federal
Existing Wild and Scenic Rivers
Study Wild and Scenic Rivers

A water management technique is used to attain one or more water-derived services. Some of these services are attained by investing large sums of labor, capital, and management; other services require little of these; and still others may require social controls that regulate other uses of water and/or related lands. Combinations of these techniques are becoming increasingly common. The most common technique is the so-called engineering approach which usually employs structures to physically control the movement of water. Man manipulates nature to achieve goals. Many of the services noted above were developed by this method. When these structures are built by the federal government, as many are in the Pacific Northwest, a large part of the costs are nonreimbursable and are therefore particularly attractive to state and local governments. Land treatment, such as contour plowing and manipulation of vegetation in a watershed, is another type of engineering approach.

The nonstructural approach, which received little attention until recently, employs social controls and may be used to complement structures. For example, floodplain zoning would complement dams and levees, and the enforcement of water quality standards or a system of discharge permits would make low flow augmentation from reservoirs more effective to abate pollution.

The map of management techniques depicts both engineering and nonstructural techniques, although the former is conspicuously dominant. Even the land treatment projects by the Soil Conservation Service may include dams. Conversely, the National Wild and Scenic River System illustrates the nonstructural approach. Three of the eight U. S. rivers designated for the system in 1968 are in the region. Rivers in the study category are undergoing thorough appraisal to determine whether they will be included in the system. In addition, Oregon has a State Scenic Waterways System (not mapped) and Washington is considering the establishment of one.

The nameplate° rating of hydropower plants associated with the dams may be seen on the map of electric generating facilities. An even greater proportion of the structures are publicly owned than the maps of generating facilities and management techniques would indicate. A large proportion of those structures classified as nonfederal were built by public utilities, a notable example being six dams on the main stem of the Columbia. Significant privately owned power developments are on the central Snake, Deschutes, Clackamas, and Lewis rivers. Many of the reservoirs in the region are popular attractions for tourists and recreationists. The record of visitations at the federal reservoirs is shown below. Some are primarily tourist attractions while others are visited largely by recreationists seeking water-oriented activities.

° The actual capacities of generating units often exceed nameplate ratings by 15%.

RECREATIONAL USE OF MAJOR FEDERAL RESERVOIRS, 1970

Corps of Engineers Projects					Bureau of Reclamation Projects				
Dam or reservoir	Total visitations	Camp and picnic	Sight-seeing	All others°	Dam or reservoir	Total visitations	Camp and picnic	Sight-seeing	All others°
	1,000	*Percent*	*Percent*	*Percent*		*1,000*	*Percent*	*Percent*	*Percent*
Washington-Oregon					*Washington*				
Bonneville	3,311,991	6.6	56.7	36.7	Banks Lake	235,422	9.3	65.8	24.9
The Dalles	464,244	37.9	49.6	12.5	Franklin D. Roosevelt	660,000	33.2	35.8	31.0
John Day	50,829	.3	99.0	.7	Grand Coulee Dam	402,000	......	100	......
McNary	3,635,835	24.5	48.0	27.5	Potholes	264,498	27.4	4.0	68.6
					Conconully	117,150	78.0	10.0	12.0
Washington					Bumping Lake	70,400	32.0	15.6	52.4
Lake Rufus Woods	72,006	14.8	69.7	15.5	Clear Creek	57,235	54.2	28.8	17.0
Mud Mountain	38,773	3.2	96.8	......	Cle Elum	30,700	26.4	42.0	31.6
Ice Harbor	465,993	27.9	23.5	48.6	Easton Diversion	145,147	84.9	7.8	7.3
Lower Monumental	143,588	14.0	39.3	46.7	Kachess	75,800	59.8	14.0	26.2
Mill Creek	127,997	23.1	38.1	38.8	Rimrock Lake	154,225	17.0	77.8	5.2
Oregon					*Oregon*				
Blue River	66,505	2.9	83.8	13.3	Phillips Lake	64,300	74.8	7.6	17.6
Cottage Grove	180,460	32.2	25.9	41.9	Crescent Lake	73,650	33.5	16.3	50.2
Cougar	220,325	15.4	41.3	43.3	Ochoco	262,300	40.7	9.1	50.2
Detroit	635,197	32.9	25.6	41.5	Prineville	271,213	6.1	5.3	88.6
Dexter-Lookout Point	349,405	19.6	43.0	37.4	Crane Prairie	85,150	64.4	28.2	7.4
Dorena	204,670	16.3	28.9	54.8	Wickiup	174,150	34.3	13.8	51.9
Fall Creek	209,200	12.5	35.9	51.6	Owyhee	188,400	6.7	21.2	72.1
Fern Ridge	1,435,270	17.1	38.6	44.3	Agate	98,000	23.5	20.4	56.1
Green Peter-Foster	427,980	13.2	40.4	46.4	Emigrant	251,300	33.4	13.5	53.1
Hills Creek	169,240	23.8	21.8	54.4	Howard Prairie	421,000	47.1	8.6	44.3
					Hyatt Prairie	138,500	20.0	21.7	58.3
Idaho					Bully Creek	28,300	12.4	10.6	77.0
Albeni Falls	315,620	24.2	30.7	45.1					
Lucky Peak	1,983,180	13.9	19.2	66.9	*Idaho*				
					Anderson Ranch	25,100	20.7	31.9	47.4
					Black Canyon	33,000	51.5	18.2	30.3
					Cascade	122,864	65.1	9.4	25.5
					Lake Lowell	209,926	17.2	30.6	52.2
					American Falls	49,720	10.1	16.5	73.4
					Island Park	94,800	51.3	12.7	36.0
					Palisades Reservoir	229,580	9.2	78.4	12.4

° Includes boating, fishing, hunting, water skiing, and swimming.

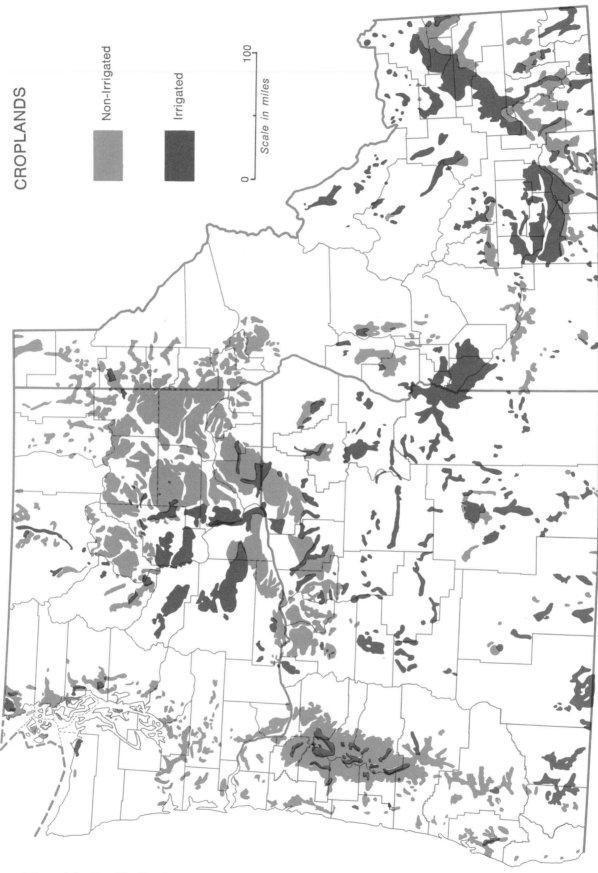

CROPLANDS

Non-Irrigated

Irrigated

0   100
Scale in miles

Agriculture ————————————————————————— Richard M. Highsmith, Jr.

OREGON, WASHINGTON, AND IDAHO combine to account for slightly more than 4% of the nation's cash receipts derived from farming. The region shows a greater emphasis on crops than does the nation. Recently the regional ratio has been about 56 to 44 in favor of crops, whereas the nation has been about 60 to 40 in favor of livestock products.

Although three crops—wheat, hay, and barley—occupy 80% of the cropland harvested, fifty crops bring annual income in excess of $100,000 to northwest farmers. The region is outstanding in the national production pattern of hops, peppermint, dry peas, snap beans, fall Irish potatoes, several grass seeds, apples, winter pears, sweet cherries, bush berries, and filberts.

The organization of agriculture in the region is following the national trend: decline in farm numbers, increase in farm size, and increase in farm inputs other than land and labor.

The accompanying maps and graphs depict the main characteristics and patterns of agriculture in the region. The principal source of data is the 1969 Census of Agriculture.

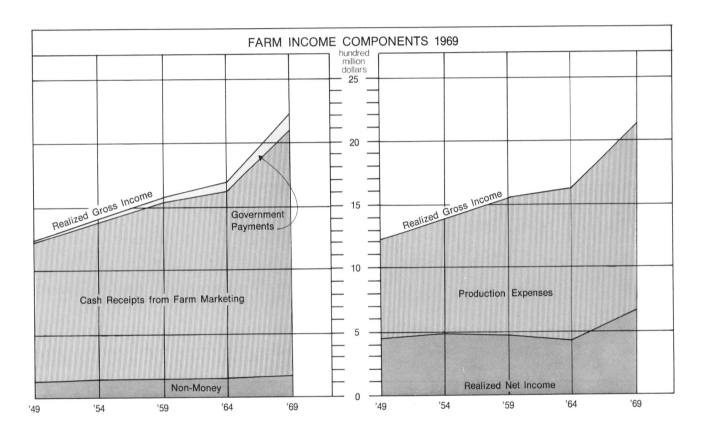

FARMLAND IN THE PACIFIC NORTHWEST, 1969
In Thousands of Acres

Item	Oregon	Washington	Idaho	Total
Cropland harvested	2,894	4,367	3,955	11,216
Cropland only pastured	1,077	834	967	2,878
Other cropland	1,227	3,029	1,251	5,507
Total Cropland	5,198	8,230	6,172	19,591
Woodland in farms	2,039	3,108	972	6,111
Other land in farms	10,789	6,221	7,270	24,280
Total cropland	18,018	17,559	14,417	49,994
Percentage of states in farms	29.3%	41.2%	27.2%	31.8%
Percentage of farmland in cropland	28.8%	46.9%	42.8%	39.2%
Irrigated land in farms	1,519	1,224	2,761	5,504

SOURCE: 1969 Census of Agriculture.

AGRICULTURAL TRENDS 1959-1969

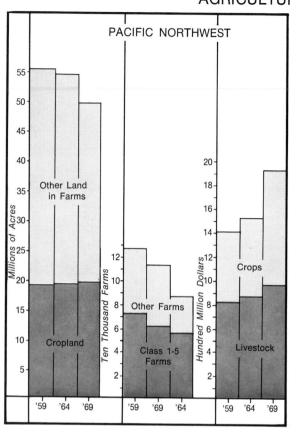

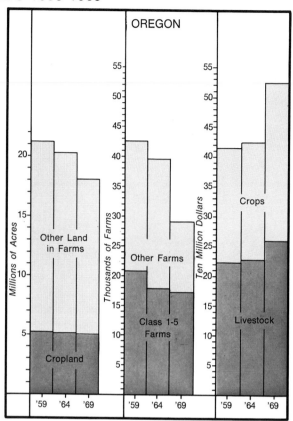

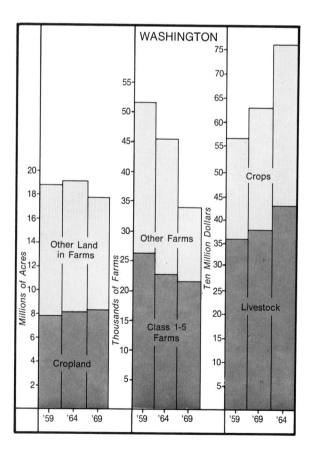

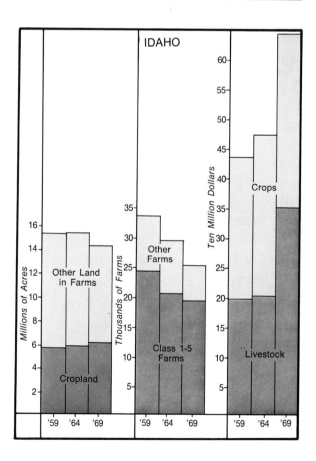

LAND IN FARMS

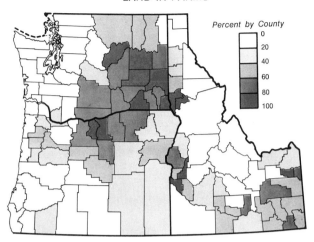

Percent by County

0
20
40
60
80
100

FARMS—SALES OVER $2,500

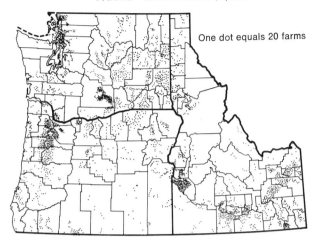

One dot equals 20 farms

FARMS—SALES UNDER $2,500

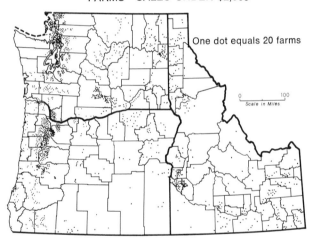

One dot equals 20 farms

0   100
Scale in Miles

FARMS—SALES OVER $40,000

One dot equals 20 farms

AVERAGE FARM SIZE, Class 1-5

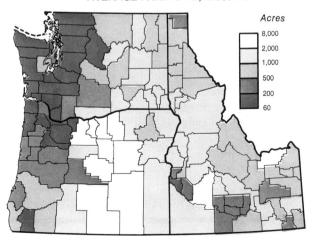

Acres

8,000
2,000
1,000
500
200
60

NUMBER OF FARMS BY INCOME CLASS, 1969

Class—Sales of	Oregon	Washington	Idaho
1—$40,000 and over	3,058	4,349	3,152
2—$20,000 to $39,999	3,096	4,835	4,251
3—$10,000 to $19,999	3,254	4,474	4,870
4—$5,000 to $9,999	3,520	3,884	4,022
5—$2,500 to $4,999	4,075	4,246	3,210
Other	12,060	12,245	5,970
Total farms	29,063	34,033	25,475

Agriculture   79

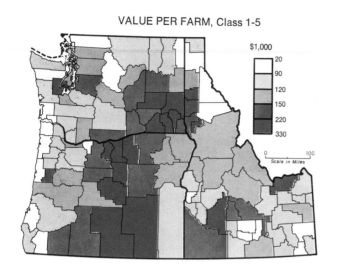

VALUE PER FARM, Class 1-5

$1,000
20
90
120
150
220
330

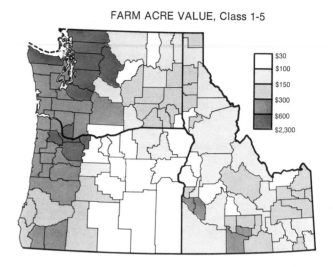

FARM ACRE VALUE, Class 1-5

$30
$100
$150
$300
$600
$2,300

FARM INCOME COMPONENTS 1969

by producing areas

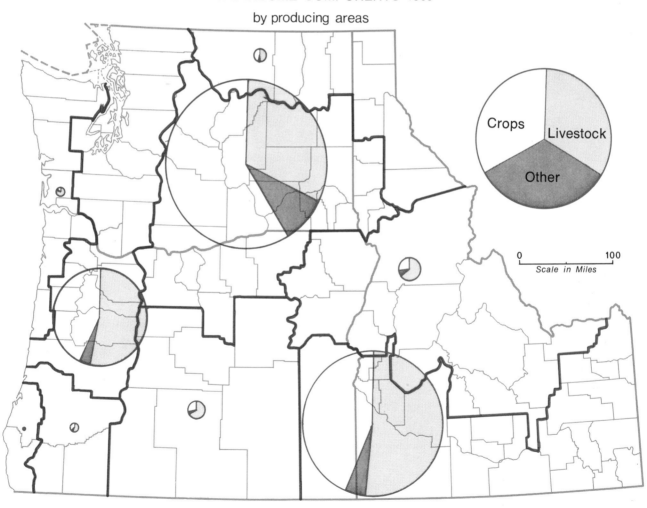

Crops   Livestock

Other

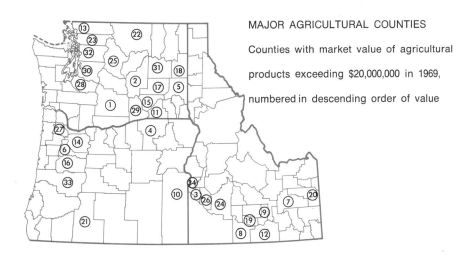

MAJOR AGRICULTURAL COUNTIES

Counties with market value of agricultural

products exceeding $20,000,000 in 1969,

numbered in descending order of value

KEY TO MAP NUMBERS
Counties with Market Value of Agricultural Products Exceeding $20,000,000, 1969

		Total	Crops	Livestock
1.	Yakima, Washington	$137,725,509	$83,747,595	$53,801,470
2.	Grant, Washington	80,654,809	44,078,511	36,575,298
3.	Canyon, Idaho	76,634,823	37,415,736	39,218,937
4.	Umatilla, Oregon	54,323,101	20,529,791	33,662,935
5.	Whitman, Washington	48,232,939	40,088,692	8,107,836
6.	Marion, Oregon	48,223,850	34,940,360	12,841,613
7.	Bingham, Idaho	47,390,883	25,815,467	21,548,781
8.	Twin Falls, Idaho	47,109,840	23,602,065	23,507,125
9.	Minidoka, Idaho	47,092,478	17,281,784	29,810,694
10.	Malheur, Oregon	43,105,014	23,040,163	20,063,573
11.	Walla Walla, Washington	35,865,488	23,775,917	12,067,974
12.	Cassia, Idaho	35,242,681	17,277,742	17,964,079
13.	Whatcom, Washington	33,895,038	5,666,401	28,118,789
14.	Clackamas, Oregon	32,865,740	13,445,746	18,546,328
15.	Franklin, Washington	32,331,771	25,691,400	6,640,371
16.	Linn, Oregon	31,388,825	20,911,477	10,236,005
17.	Adams, Washington	30,686,844	22,723,762	7,962,393
18.	Spokane, Washington	29,744,300	16,913,932	12,692,411
19.	Jerome, Idaho	28,768,069	11,889,226	16,878,843
20.	Bonneville, Idaho	27,591,092	16,548,325	11,042,767
21.	Klamath, Oregon	27,371,745	10,790,408	16,348,822
22.	Okanogan, Washington	26,293,877	18,005,594	7,965,862
23.	Skagit, Washington	26,234,667	11,937,541	14,277,430
24.	Elmore, Idaho	24,632,318	7,178,993	17,450,724
25.	Chelan, Washington	24,107,516	23,736,519	412,394
26.	Ada, Idaho	23,823,593	5,494,561	18,328,457
27.	Washington, Oregon	23,435,487	15,475,827	7,775,611
28.	Pierce, Washington	22,960,966	6,045,195	16,720,871
29.	Benton, Washington	22,833,323	15,733,893	7,099,430
30.	King, Washington	22,388,965	6,951,572	15,405,667
31.	Lincoln, Washington	22,221,170	16,770,840	5,337,872
32.	Snohomish, Washington	21,900,415	2,992,360	18,788,689
33.	Lane, Oregon	21,653,227	11,780,769	9,319,416
34.	Payette, Idaho	21,153,603	4,608,421	16,544,817

SOURCE: 1969 Census of Agriculture.
Total includes farm sales of forest products.

Agriculture 81

WHEAT

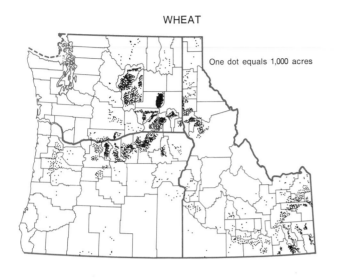

One dot equals 1,000 acres

BARLEY

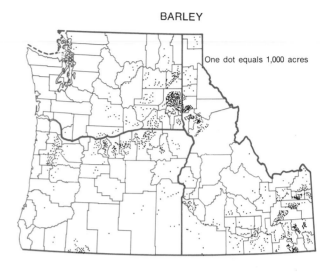

One dot equals 1,000 acres

OATS

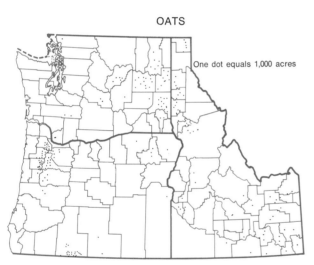

One dot equals 1,000 acres

FIELD CORN

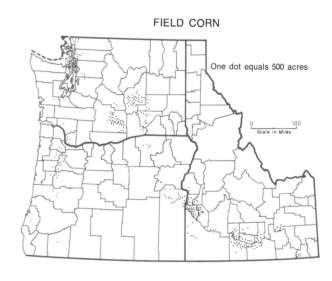

One dot equals 500 acres

Scale in Miles
0 ___ 100

ALFALFA AND ALFALFA MIXTURES

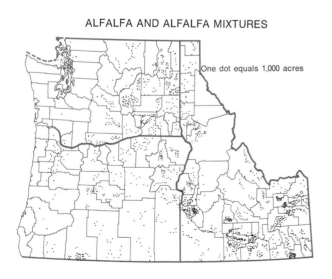

One dot equals 1,000 acres

OTHER HAY CROPS

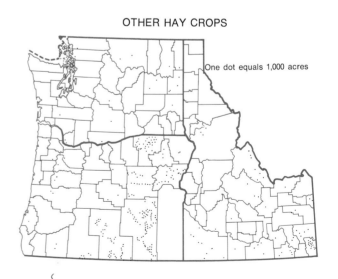

One dot equals 1,000 acres

FIELD SEEDS

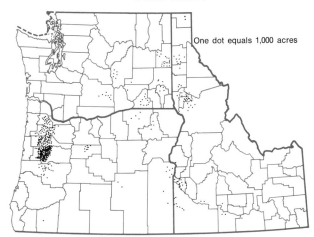

One dot equals 1,000 acres

ALL VEGETABLES

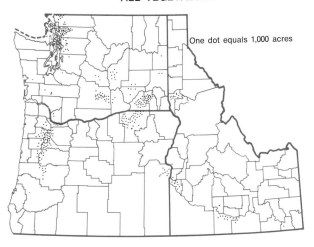

One dot equals 1,000 acres

SWEET CORN

One dot equals 1,000 acres

SNAP BEANS

One dot equals 500 acres

POTATOES

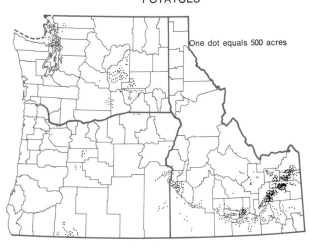

One dot equals 500 acres

STRAWBERRIES

One dot equals 500 acres

Agriculture   83

LAND IN ORCHARDS

One dot equals 1,000 acres

APPLES

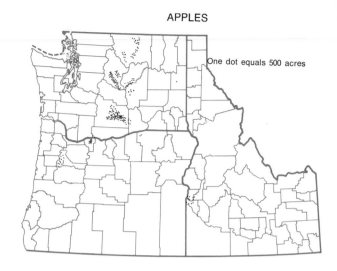

One dot equals 500 acres

PEARS

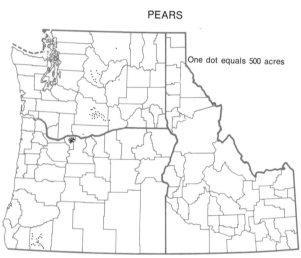

One dot equals 500 acres

PEACHES

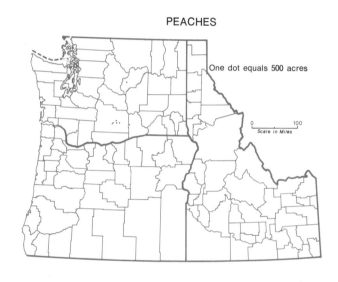

One dot equals 500 acres

Scale in Miles
0   100

CHERRIES

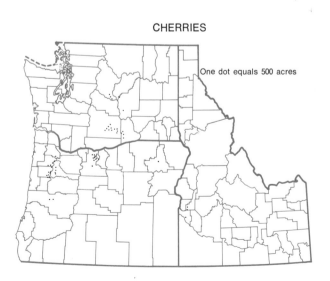

One dot equals 500 acres

GRAPES

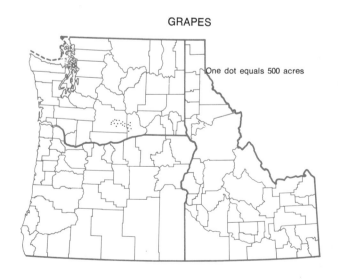

One dot equals 500 acres

IMPROVED PASTURE

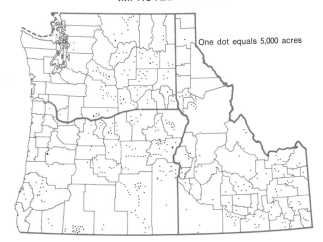

One dot equals 5,000 acres

CROPLAND USED AS PASTURE

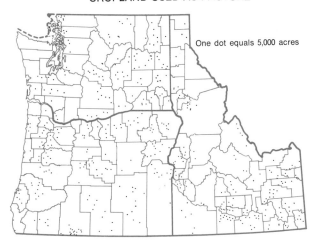

One dot equals 5,000 acres

CATTLE AND CALVES

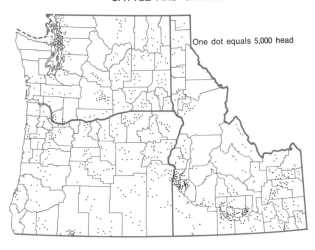

One dot equals 5,000 head

MILK COWS

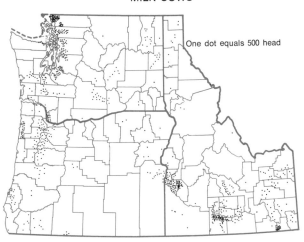

One dot equals 500 head

HOGS AND PIGS

One dot equals 1,000 head

SHEEP AND LAMBS

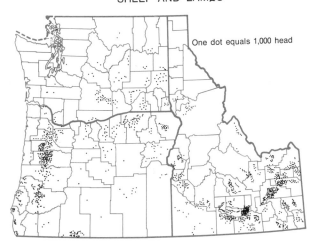

One dot equals 1,000 head

LAYING-AGE CHICKENS

One dot equals 30,000 birds

0   100
Scale in Miles

BROILERS AND OTHER MEAT-TYPE CHICKENS

One dot equals 30,000 birds

FARM COMMODITY SALES 1969

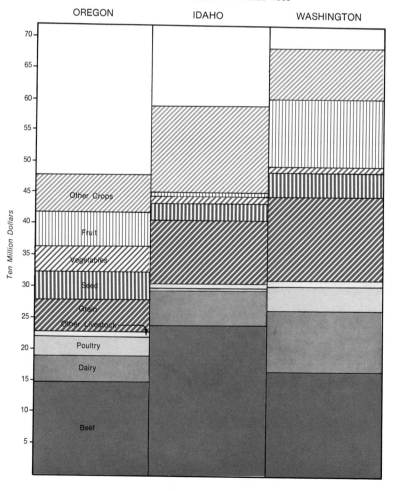

OREGON   IDAHO   WASHINGTON

Ten Million Dollars

70 —
65 —
60 —
55 —
50 —
45 —
40 —
35 —
30 —
25 —
20 —
15 —
10 —
5 —

Other Crops

Fruit

Vegetables

Seed

Grain

Other Livestock

Poultry

Dairy

Beef

▲ SUNNYSIDE CANAL, Yakima Project, irrigating orchards and dairy operations

COLUMBIA BASIN ▶ PROJECT. Quincy Valley, Washington; West Canal left foreground

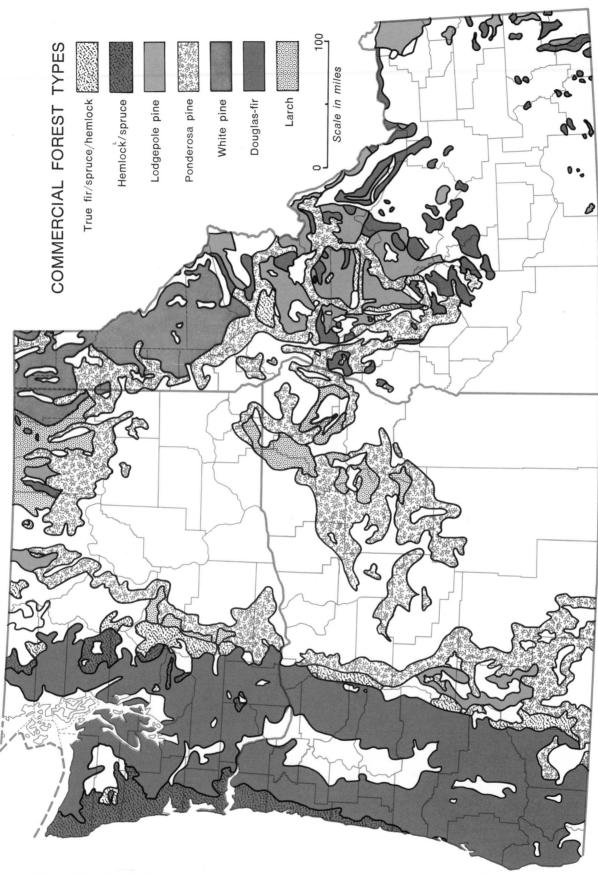

COMMERCIAL FOREST TYPES

True fir/spruce/hemlock

Hemlock/spruce

Lodgepole pine

Ponderosa pine

White pine

Douglas-fir

Larch

Scale in miles

0   100

Forest Resources and Industries ———————————————— J. Granville Jensen

WITH 12% of the nation's commercial forest lands, the Pacific Northwest accounts for about 35% of the total standing timber resource and provides about 25% of the annual wood harvest. The associated primary forest industries supply two-thirds of the nation's plywood, a third of the lumber, and 17% of the wood pulp for paper, board, and other products.

Commercial forest lands account for 39% of the Pacific Northwest but the distribution is uneven. The mild, winter-wet area west of the Cascade Mountains is about 75% commercial forest land, dominated by stands of Douglas-fir type forest (Douglas-fir Subregion). East of the Cascades, tree-growing conditions are less favorable and commercial forest lands occupy only 30% of the total land area, and these are associated with the more humid higher elevations. Pine species predominate so the area is commonly termed the Western Pine Subregion, although considerable Douglas-fir grows on higher elevations.

Forest lands of the Pacific Northwest have been recognized as having national resource significance and large areas have been incorporated into the National Forest System. The resultant fact that over half of the commercial forest lands are in federal ownership has important implications for the regional economy and for forest management.

Natural productivity of the forest lands is high in the Douglas-fir subregion, and less than 20% of the land is poorly stocked. Thus the area west of the Cascades, with only 5% of the nation's commercial forest lands, accounts for 37% of the nation's class-one forest land. Nearly 65% of the Pacific Northwest sawtimber volume and 28% of the nation's is in the Douglas-fir Subregion. The private forest lands, accounting for about half of the total in the subregion, are predominantly high productivity lands. In contrast, nearly 75% of the Western Pine Subregion is low productivity land.

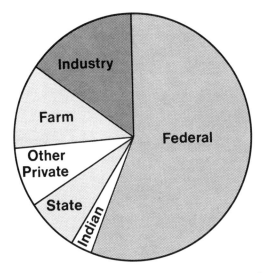

COMMERCIAL FOREST LAND AREA
By Ownership

AREA OF COMMERCIAL FOREST LANDS BY FOREST TYPES
Thousands of Acres*

Area	Total	Douglas-fir	Hemlock spruce	Ponderosa pine	Fir/ Spruce	Lodgepole pine	White pine	Larch	Hardwoods
Douglas-fir Subregion	26,032†	15,420	4,265	162	2,023	192	224	4	3,732
Washington	10,950	5,711	2,899	3	990	46	26	..	1,275
Oregon	15,082†	9,709	1,366	159	1,033	146	198	4	2,457
Pine Subregion	35,914	8,881	167	13,509	3,633	5,163	2,343	1,589	629
Washington	8,560	2,972	......	3,467	744	732	111	471	63
Oregon	11,531	1,111	......	7,418	1,134	1,408	54	388	18
Idaho	15,823	4,798	167	2,624	1,755	3,023	2,178	730	548
Totals	61,946	24,301	4,432	13,671	5,656	5,355	2,567	1,593	4,361

* Timber Trends in the United States, USDA Forest Service, 1965 and Timber Resources Statistics for the Pacific Northwest, PNW-9, USDA Forest Service, 1965.
† Includes 10,000 acres redwood forest type in southwestern Oregon.

Site classes 1 and 2
Site class 3
Site class 4

FOREST LAND PRODUCTIVITY

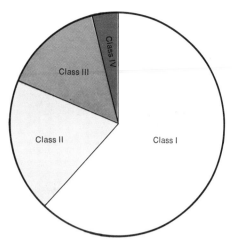

Class IV

Class III

Class II

Class I

Douglas-fir region
land productivity classes in
cubic feet growth per acre per year

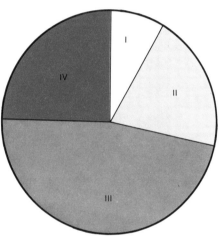

I

II

IV

III

Pine region
land productivity classes in
cubic feet per acre per year

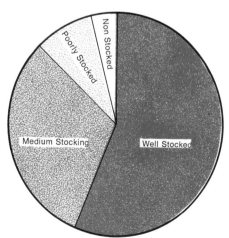

Non Stocked

Poorly Stocked

Medium Stocking

Well Stocked

Commercial forest land condition
Adequacy of tree stocking

90   Atlas of the Pacific Northwest

VOLUME OF STANDING TIMBER AND TIMBER HARVESTED 1970
By Ownership

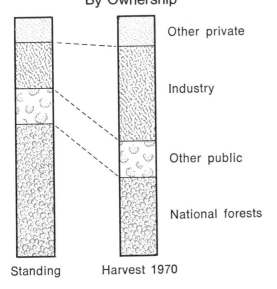

Other private

Industry

Other public

National forests

Standing   Harvest 1970

About 70% of the timber harvest of the Pacific Northwest is in counties west of the Cascade Mountains. Douglas and Lane counties of southwestern Oregon are especially significant, each producing about 1½ billion board feet annual harvest to account for 17% of the regional total. The forest lands owned by private industry account for about 40% of the annual harvest. In recent years nearly half of the annual harvest is utilized for lumber, about 20% for veneer, 25% for pulpwood, and 7% for log exports.

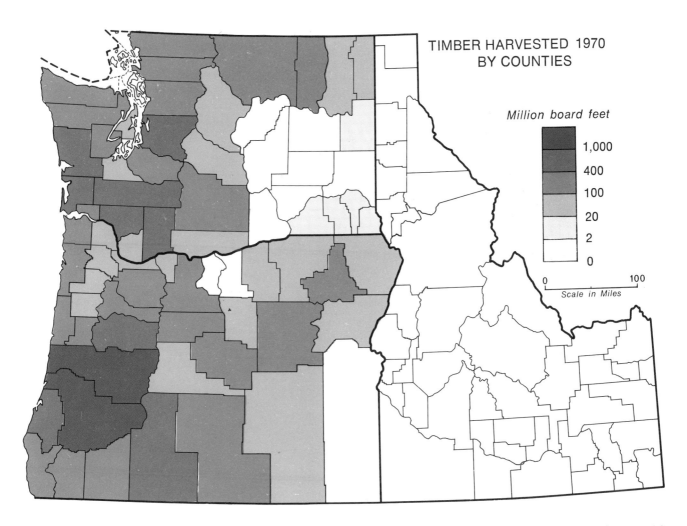

TIMBER HARVESTED 1970
BY COUNTIES

Million board feet

1,000
400
100
20
2
0

0   100
Scale in Miles

Location of primary forest industries correlates closely with harvest areas as transport costs of the bulky raw materials are restrictive. Thus primary mills west of the Cascades account for about 70% of total wood consumption. Timber utilization, however, differs considerably from area to area. Western Washington mills predominantly are oriented to pulp and paper production and account for about 60% of pulpwood consumption of the Pacific Northwest. In contrast the western Oregon industry is dominated by consumption of timber for veneer and lumber, accounting for about 60% of all veneer log consumption.

Sawmills are almost ubiquitous, being widely distributed throughout the forest areas of the Pacific Northwest. For the most part their location has resulted from proximity to available timber and road access since most logs are transported by truck. Although a few large integrated mills are able to utilize all log types, the recent trend is to sort logs in the woods for highest potential and to route them to appropriate converting centers for veneer, lumber, or pulp.

Softwood plywood production is about 70% from western Oregon, especially the southern counties, having gradually migrated southward from western Washington in response to changing availability of veneer logs.

The region's pulpmill locations are also raw material oriented, although they strongly reveal the importance of available water and the stabilizing effect of larger capital investment. Although the pulp industry started in western Oregon, currently about 60% of the region's pulp mill capacity is concentrated in the lowlands of western Washington fronting Puget Sound and the Columbia River. Since 1950 pulp mills have increasingly utilized wood residue of sawmills and planing mills, and recent estimates suggest that as much as two-thirds of all wood consumed in pulp mills is chips transported by truck and rail from other processing mills.

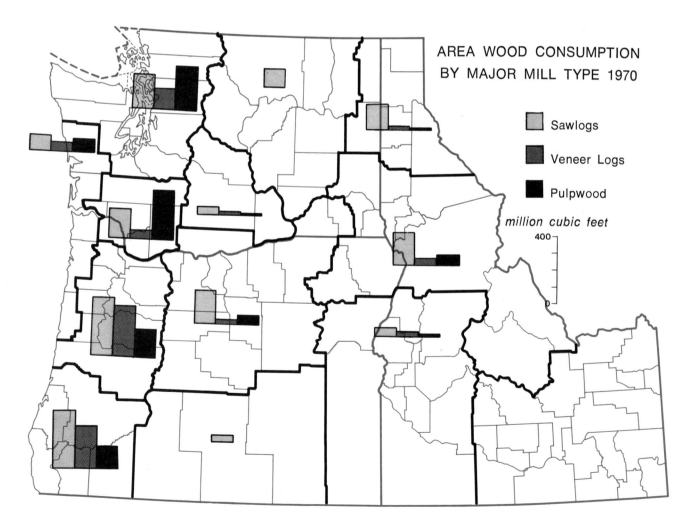

AREA WOOD CONSUMPTION
BY MAJOR MILL TYPE 1970

Sawlogs

Veneer Logs

Pulpwood

million cubic feet

400

0

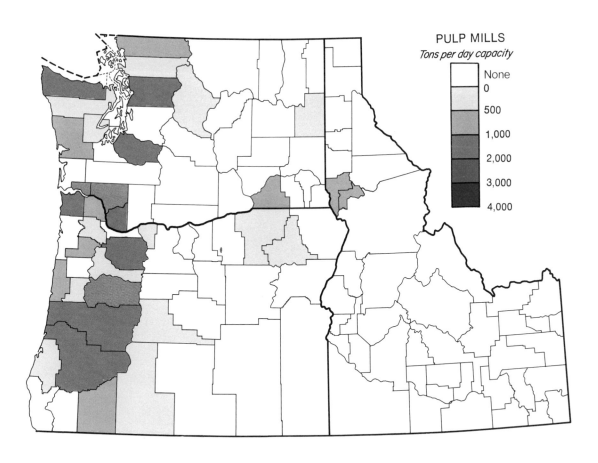

PULP MILLS
Tons per day capacity

None
0
500
1,000
2,000
3,000
4,000

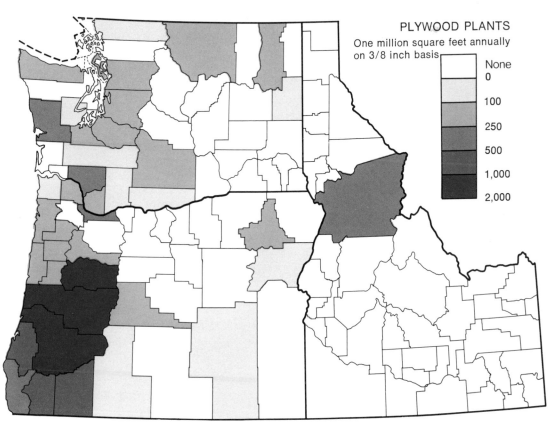

PLYWOOD PLANTS
One million square feet annually
on 3/8 inch basis

None
0
100
250
500
1,000
2,000

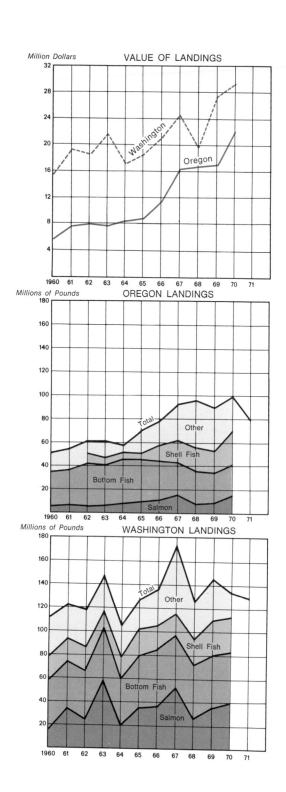

Million Dollars

VALUE OF LANDINGS

Millions of Pounds

OREGON LANDINGS

Millions of Pounds

WASHINGTON LANDINGS

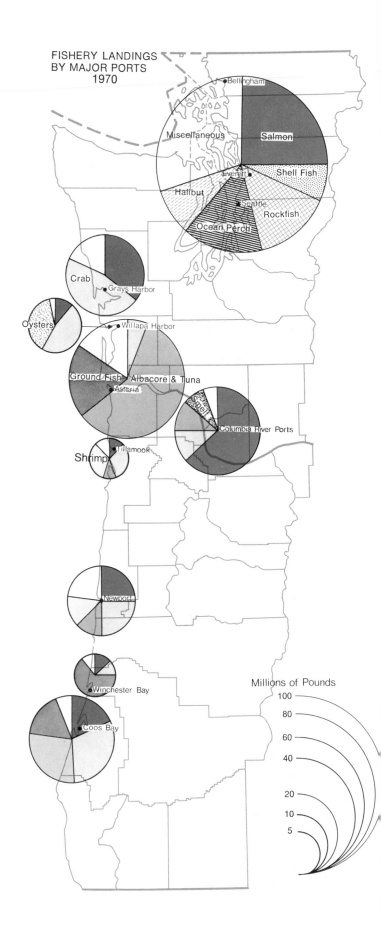

FISHERY LANDINGS
BY MAJOR PORTS
1970

Millions of Pounds
100
80
60
40
20
10
5

Fisheries Resources ———————————————————————— J. Granville Jensen

COMMERCIAL FISHERIES RESOURCES of the Pacific Northwest are generous both in variety and in quantity, support a significant industry, and in some sectors have potentials for further development. Landings in 1970 accounted for 5% of the United States total and for 9% of the value.

Anadromous salmon constitute the region's most highly regarded fish resource and account for about 25% of the harvest and 50% of the value in most years. Annual landings by species vary considerably, especially the Pink salmon of Puget Sound waters. About 90% of salmon harvested are taken within the three-mile zone. Major conservation efforts including artificial spawning appear to be having success in maintaining salmon runs.

Bottom fisheries include 30-40 species, especially flounders and "sole," ocean perch, lingcod, and rockfishes. A significant portion of the catch is taken outside of the 12-mile limit. The halibut fishery is mainly in northern Washington waters and landings include fish from the North Pacific. Overfishing of halibut led to international agreement for rigorous constraints that have resulted in rebuilding the stocks of this highly regarded species.

The important albacore tuna fishery is largely off Oregon waters and southward. Notable receipts at Astoria, including landings from vessels harvesting in distant waters, support one of the region's major fish processing centers.

Shellfish resources are important both in Oregon and in Washington. Major harvests include crab from both states, shrimp especially in Oregon, oysters and clams notably from Washington waters of Willapa Bay and Puget Sound. The luxury shellfish industry very likely has potentials for expansion, but it is threatened by serious pollution problems.

Conservational management of the region's fishery resource has long been of major concern to the state agencies and national agencies. Problems have included difficulties in regulating Indian fishing in the Columbia River, the impact of dams on salmon runs, pollution, and harvest competition with vessels of other nations, especially those of the Soviet Union, Japan, and Canada. Since 1965 intensive harvest off Oregon and Washington, especially by the Soviet fishing fleet, caused concern for stocks of bottom fishes. Although the international problem of "ownership" and of fishing rights has not been resolved, negotiations between United States and Soviet representatives have resulted in agreements to limit Soviet harvest.

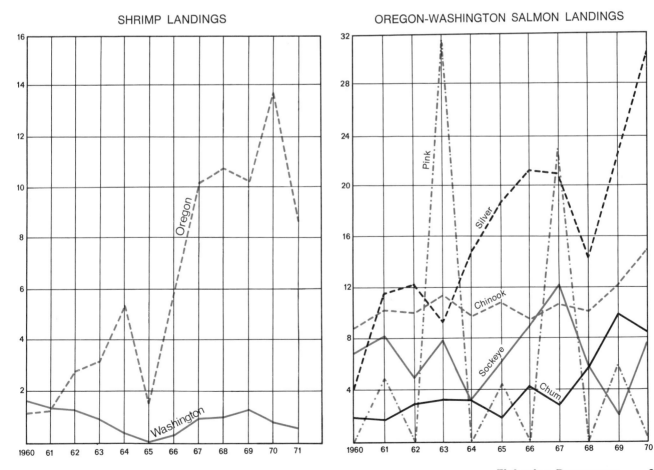

SHRIMP LANDINGS

OREGON-WASHINGTON SALMON LANDINGS

◄ COAL FIELD at Centralia, Washington, using 58-yard overburden removal dragline

GRAVEL OPERATION ▼

Minerals and Mining

Thomas J. Maresh

A VARIETY OF MINERAL RESOURCES are found throughout the Pacific Northwest, although value of production in the region does not rank it as a major national producer. In 1967, for example, Idaho, Washington, and Oregon ranked 31st, 34th, and 40th, respectively, among the states in value of mineral production. The region accounts for about 1% of the total national value of mineral production. Moreover, the mineral industries are not major employers, accounting for approximately 2% of Idaho's non-agricultural labor force, and less than .5% in Washington and Oregon.

The local importance of the mineral resource base and mineral industries is greater, however, than the above figures suggest. The map of mineral production value indicates areas in which value of output is substantial. Additionally, mine products commonly are processed, generating further employment and income in the region. Most importantly, however, mineral resources provide a base for other productive activities, such as the use of sand, gravel, and stone in building construction.

VALUE OF MINERAL PRODUCTION IN THE PACIFIC NORTHWEST
In Thousands of Dollars, 1967-70 Average

	Washington	Oregon	Idaho	Total
Cement	22,976	W	W	22,976
Clay	332	270	29*	631
Coal	572	......	......	572
Copper	16	W	3,376	3,392
Gem stones	119	750	140	1,009
Gold	W	13	138	151
Lead	1,741	W	17,605	19,346
Mercury ..	W	274	458†	732
Peat	136	......	W	136
Pumice and volcanic cinder	W	1,475	135‡	1,610
Sand, gravel, and stone	47,566	43,611	15,266	106,443
Silver	W	4	32,093	32,097
Zinc	4,055	W	15,002	19,057
Other	8,337	18,522	30,378	57,237
Total	85,850	64,919	114,620	265,389

W = data withheld.
* Excludes fire clay and kaolin; included with "other."
† 1968 data withheld.
‡ 1967 data withheld.

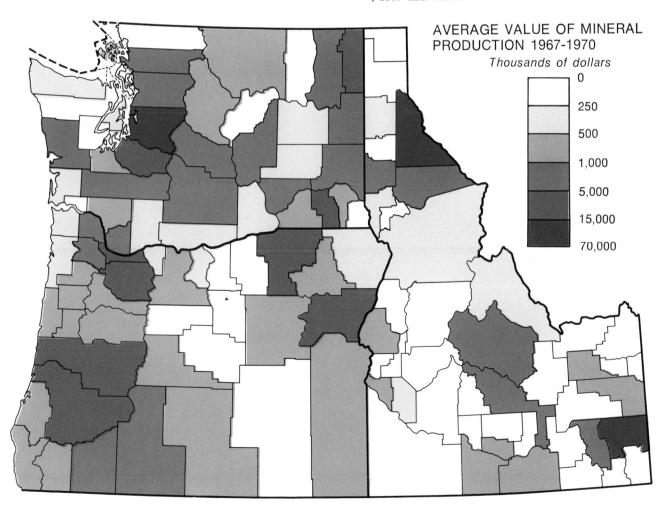

AVERAGE VALUE OF MINERAL PRODUCTION 1967-1970
Thousands of dollars

0
250
500
1,000
5,000
15,000
70,000

Mineral Production in Oregon

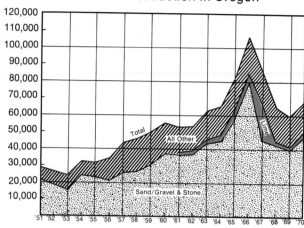

Total value of mineral production in Oregon closely parallels production of sand, gravel, and stone, which in turn reflects trends in the building industry and highway and dam construction. Lime, cement, clay, pumice and volcanic cinder, gem stones, nickel, and mercury are among the other commodities produced. As in Washington and Idaho, mineral resource potential is widespread.

Mineral Production in Washington

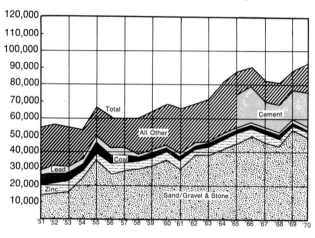

Washington has shown a steady, modest growth in value of mineral output over the past two decades. Construction materials, such as sand, gravel, and stone, as well as cement, are the most significant commodities produced. Minerals produced in lesser quantities include zinc, lead, coal, clay, copper, and peat. King County leads in production, with about one-fourth of the state's total mineral value, primarily from construction materials.

Mineral Production in Idaho

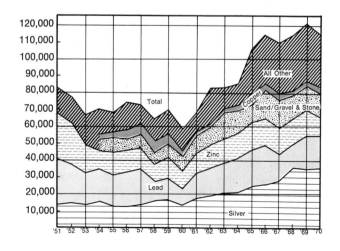

Although the mix of minerals contributing to the value of mineral production varies among the three states, all have been showing an increase in total value of production. Idaho is the region's major producer of metals, and leads in total value. It leads the nation in the production of silver, is second in lead and phosphate rock, and is third in zinc. The rich Coeur d'Alene mining district is responsible for Shoshone County being the region's leading mineral producer.

INDUSTRIAL MINERALS

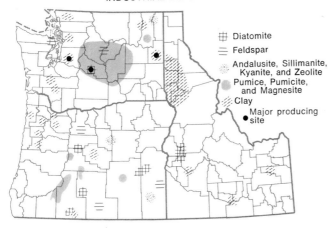

Diatomite

Feldspar

Andalusite, Sillimanite, Kyanite, and Zeolite

Pumice, Pumicite, and Magnesite

Clay

● Major producing site

The major industrial minerals—sand, gravel, and stone—are produced at sites distributed throughout the region. These sites are too numerous to be shown. Transportation costs constitute an important share of delivered costs, with the result that most consumption takes place within 25 miles of the point of production. Land use restrictions and urban expansion have, in some localities, prohibited development of sand and gravel resources.

Selected location of resource potential for a variety of other nonmetals are shown on the adjacent map. Data for locational maps were provided by U. S. Bureau of Mines liaison officers in each state.

Washington, which contains most of the region's coal reserves, reached its peak production in 1918, with 4,082,000 tons. In recent years production has declined markedly, with only 37,000 tons being produced in 1970, from one strip mine in Lewis County and two underground mines in King County. With the completion of a 1.4 million kilowatt coal-fired electric plant near Centralia, production is again increasing. Annual consumption is expected to reach 4.8 million tons.

COAL

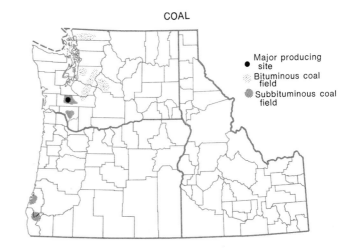

● Major producing site

Bituminous coal field

Subbituminous coal field

PETROLEUM AND GEOTHERMAL POTENTIAL

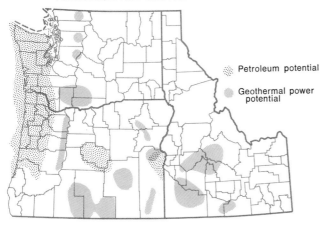

Petroleum potential

Geothermal power potential

Although the Pacific Northwest is not a producer of petroleum, the potential of production has resulted in a number of exploratory ventures and test drills over recent years and continues to attract interest. Increasing demands for energy in the region and concern for the economic and environmental costs of deriving energy from various sources also have led to growing interest in tapping the geothermal energy potential of the area.

Minerals and Mining 99

BAUXITE AND TITANIUM POTENTIAL

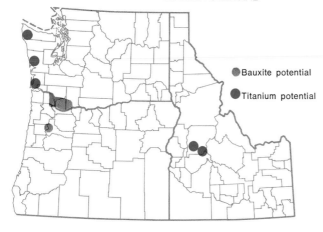

Bauxite and titanium deposits are known to exist in the area, but are not presently developed. The bauxite deposits of the Willamette Valley have been tested for possible use in the aluminum industry, but they are not competitive with sources outside the Pacific Northwest.

MERCURY PRODUCTION AND PRICE

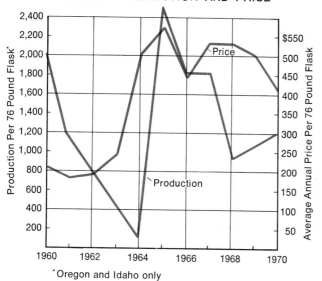

*Oregon and Idaho only

MERCURY AND URANIUM

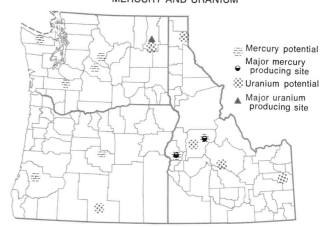

FERROUS METALS POTENTIAL

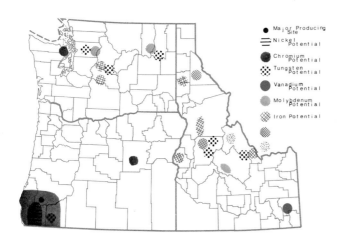

Although the Pacific Northwest has the potential for producing iron as well as a number of ferroalloys, only nickel is produced in significant quantities. Hanna Mining Company operates the nation's only domestic nickel mine, in Douglas County, Oregon. Vanadium is recovered from phosphate rock produced in Idaho, and small amounts of tungsten and iron ore have been mined in recent years.

COPPER, LEAD, AND ZINC

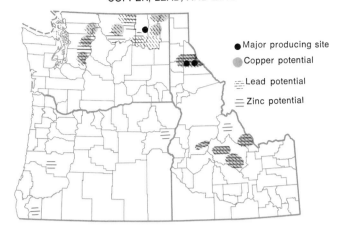

- ● Major producing site
- ⬤ Copper potential
- ≡ Lead potential
- ≡ Zinc potential

The Pacific Northwest is an important producer of lead and zinc, most of which is produced in Shoshone County, Idaho. The Coeur d'Alene mining district in that county has produced since the 1860's, and has accounted for approximately 6.8 million tons of lead and 2.4 million tons of zinc. Most of the copper produced in the Pacific Northwest comes from complex ores in association with such metals as lead, zinc, gold, and silver.

GOLD AND SILVER

The Pacific Northwest is the nation's major producer of silver, with more production in Idaho than all other states of the nation combined. Production centers on the Coeur d'Alene district, where the Sunshine mine is the nation's largest producer. Most of the gold produced comes as a by-product from complex ores in the same district, with the Lucky Friday mine producing 42% of the state's total. Lesser amounts of gold and silver are produced in the Republic district in Ferry County, Washington.

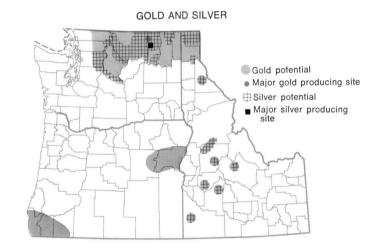

- ⬤ Gold potential
- ● Major gold producing site
- ⊞ Silver potential
- ■ Major silver producing site

INDUSTRY IN OREGON
(above) Astoria with fish cannery left of the bridge
(left) Oregon city, pulp and paper center
(below) Integrated wood-products milling center at Springfield

INDUSTRY IN WASHINGTON
(above) Aluminum plant at Vancouver
(right) Seattle industrial district
(below) Copper smelter and refinery at
Ruston near Tacoma

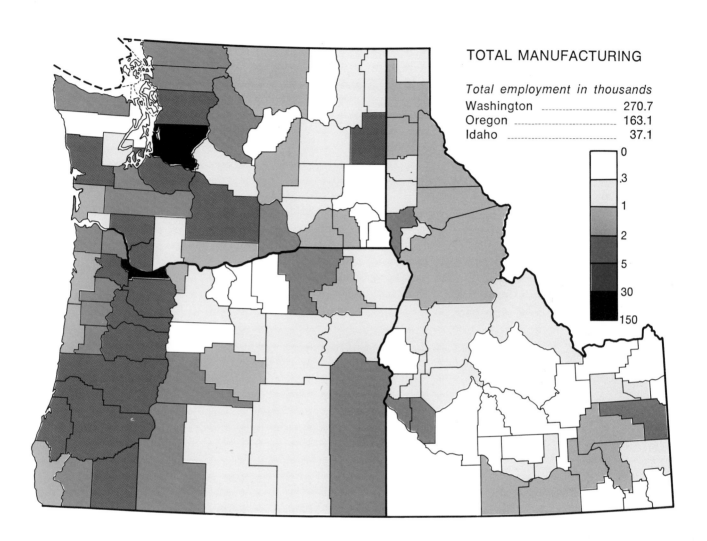

TOTAL MANUFACTURING

Total employment in thousands
Washington ⸺⸺⸺⸺⸺ 270.7
Oregon ⸺⸺⸺⸺⸺⸺ 163.1
Idaho ⸺⸺⸺⸺⸺⸺ 37.1

0
.3
1
2
5
30
150

Manufacturing ——————————————————————— Thomas J. Maresh

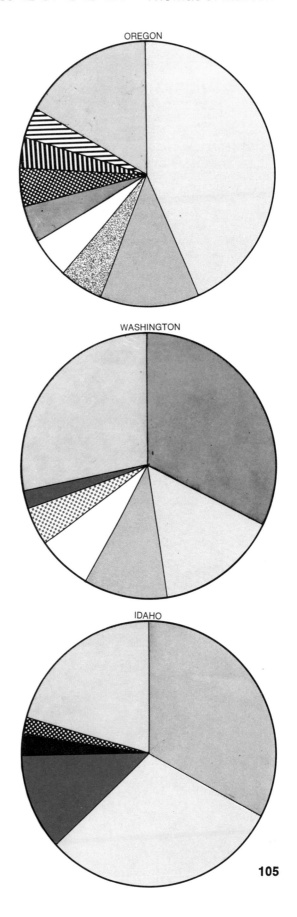

THE 1967 CENSUS OF MANUFACTURES reported 470,900 persons employed in manufacturing in the Pacific Northwest, up significantly from 400,000 in 1963 and 366,600 in 1959. As can be seen on the map of total manufacturing employment, there are important spatial variations in the pattern of manufacturing employment in the region. Additionally, as shown on the graphs of manufacturing employment structure in each state, there is important variation in the composition of manufacturing. The composition of manufacturing is significant in explaining the growth of manufacturing in an area, as well as being important in terms of the economic stability of an area.

In each of the three states the various manufacturing sectors take on different levels of importance. "Lumber and wood products" is important to all three, for example, but is the most important sector in Oregon. "Transportation equipment" is the most important sector in Washington, yet is relatively insignificant in Oregon and Idaho. In each of the states the three largest sectors account for over half of the manufacturing employment, and in each instance two of the three largest sectors include "lumber and wood products" and "food and kindred products."

Manufacturing sectors are based upon the Standard Industrial Classification (SIC).

MANUFACTURING EMPLOYMENT

- Transportation equipment
- Food and kindred products
- Lumber and wood products
- Electrical equipment and supplies
- Paper and allied products
- Chemicals and allied products
- Printing and publishing
- Machinery, except electrical
- Fabricated metal products
- Stone, clay, glass products
- Primary metal industries
- All Others

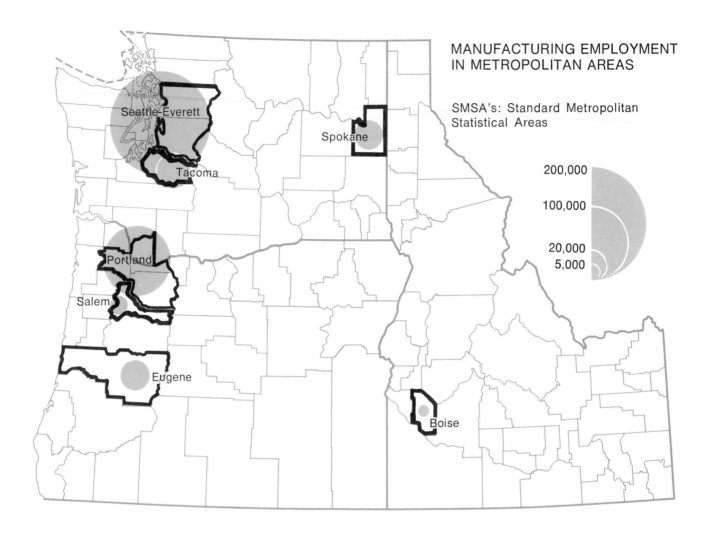

MANUFACTURING EMPLOYMENT
IN METROPOLITAN AREAS

SMSA's: Standard Metropolitan
Statistical Areas

200,000

100,000

20,000
5,000

Manufacturing is dominantly an urban activity, with agglomerations of manufacturing facilities most pronounced in the major metropolitan areas. The seven major metropolitan areas in the Pacific Northwest, shown in the above figure, account for two-thirds of the region's manufacturing employment.

The mix of manufacturing is extremely varied among these metropolitan areas. Portland is relatively diversified in its manufacturing structure, in contrast to the relatively specialized manufacturing mix of Seattle and Eugene. Specialization in one or two sectors may result in rapid expansion if those sectors are growth sectors, but may also result in high unemployment levels and local economic problems when those sectors are depressed.

As in the mix of state manufacturing employment, "food and kindred products" and "lumber and wood products" are consistently among the leading sectors in all of the metropolitan areas. However, "transportation equipment," "primary metal industries," and other sectors take on local significance.

Seattle

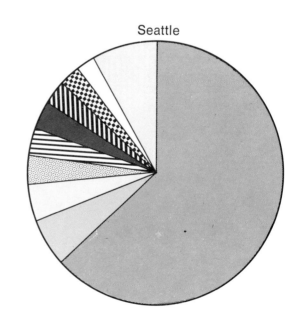

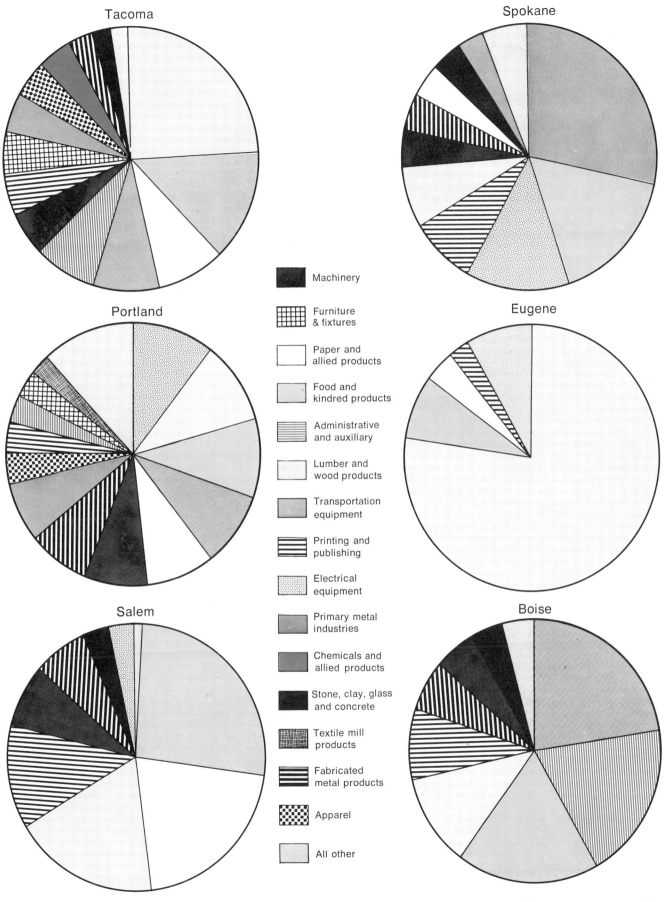

Tacoma

Spokane

Portland

Eugene

Salem

Boise

Machinery

Furniture & fixtures

Paper and allied products

Food and kindred products

Administrative and auxiliary

Lumber and wood products

Transportation equipment

Printing and publishing

Electrical equipment

Primary metal industries

Chemicals and allied products

Stone, clay, glass and concrete

Textile mill products

Fabricated metal products

Apparel

All other

SIC 33, primary metal industries, accounts for slightly less than 5% of the total manufacturing employment in the Pacific Northwest. Among the larger firms are copper, lead, and zinc smelters, iron and steel mills, and aluminum smelters and rolling mills. Included among the smaller firms are several ferroalloy plants and foundry and casting operations. Employment is dominantly in the more densely populated areas of western Washington and Oregon.

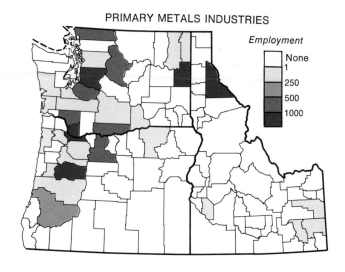

PRIMARY METALS INDUSTRIES

Employment

	None
	1
	250
	500
	1000

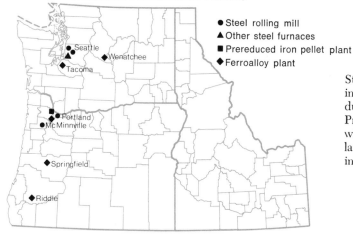

STEEL AND FERROALLOY PLANTS

● Steel rolling mill
▲ Other steel furnaces
■ Prereduced iron pellet plant
◆ Ferroalloy plant

Seattle
Tacoma
Wenatchee
Portland
McMinnville
Springfield
Riddle

Steel production in the Pacific Northwest is concentrated in Seattle and Portland. Plants are relatively small, producing mainly construction steel for the regional market. Production of steel in the area is done in electric furnaces, with most firms processing scrap metal. However, in Portland iron ore slurry imported from Peru is concentrated into pellets and then processed into steel.

The process of reducing alumina to aluminum requires the input of large quantities of electricity, a factor which has attracted smelters to sources of low-cost electricity. The location of slightly less than one-third of the nation's reduction capacity in this region is in large part explained by the relatively low-cost power advantage the region has enjoyed. This attraction may be weakening as the Pacific Northwest faces rising electricity costs.

A zinc smelter and lead smelter and refinery are operated by the Bunker Hill Company in the Coeur d'Alene district to process locally mined ores. A copper smelter and refinery operated by the American Smelting and Refining Company in Tacoma processes primarily scrap copper and imported copper concentrates.

Zirconium, titanium, and columbium are processed by several firms at Albany, Oregon.

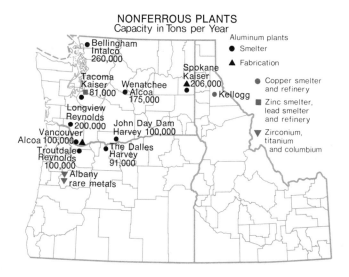

NONFERROUS PLANTS
Capacity in Tons per Year

Aluminum plants
● Smelter
▲ Fabrication

● Copper smelter and refinery
■ Zinc smelter, lead smelter and refinery
▼ Zirconium, titanium and columbium

Bellingham
Intalco
260,000
Spokane
Kaiser
206,000
Tacoma
Kaiser
81,000
Wenatchee
Alcoa
175,000
Kellogg
Longview
Reynolds
200,000
John Day Dam
Harvey 100,000
Vancouver
Alcoa 100,000
Troutdale
Reynolds
100,000
The Dalles
Harvey
91,000
Albany
rare metals

Food and kindred products (SIC 20)

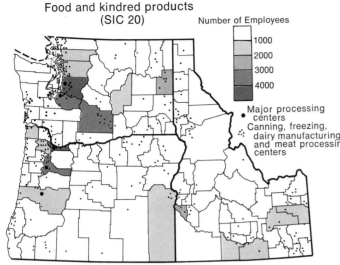

Number of Employees

1000
2000
3000
4000

● Major processing centers
Canning, freezing, dairy manufacturing and meat processing centers

"Food and kindred products" includes such activities as meat packing, dairy processing, canning and freezing, flour production, fish canning, and sugar beet processing. Although food processing is, in general, widespread through the Pacific Northwest, certain activities are localized. Dairy processing facilities and meat packing plants tend to be located near populated market areas. Activities such as sugar beet processing and fish canning are located with access to the raw foodstuff-producing areas.

Lumber and Wood Products SIC 24

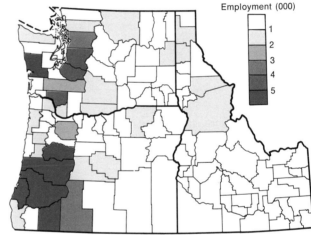

Employment (000)

1
2
3
4
5

Employment in "lumber and wood products" industries, while widespread in the Pacific Northwest, reaches its greatest importance in western Washington and Oregon. This sector presently accounts for approximately one-fourth of the manufacturing employment in the region. Recent studies suggest that employment in lumber and wood products industries will, in the future, deline in the Pacific Northwest.

Paper and Allied Products (SIC 26)

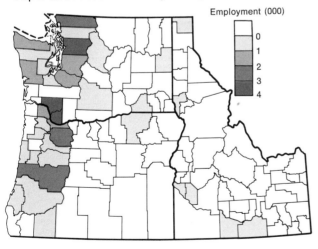

Employment (000)

0
1
2
3
4

Logging operations, sawmills, planning mills, and plywood mills are the dominant employers.

Paper mills and pulp mills account for the greatest share of the employment in SIC 26. These activities are based on the softwood resources of the region. Accordingly, plants producing paper and allied products are largely concentrated in western Washington and Oregon. Although they do not directly support a large segment of the total employment in the Pacific Northwest, they are highly significant in a number of local economies.

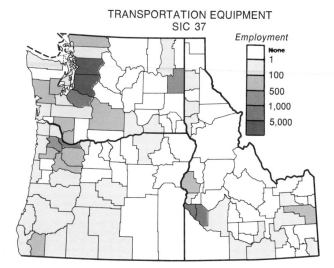

TRANSPORTATION EQUIPMENT
SIC 37

Employment
None
1
100
500
1,000
5,000

"Transportation equipment" is the leading manufacturing employment sector in Washington, and contributes significantly to the manufacturing of Seattle, Portland, Boise, and Tacoma. Aircraft, ship and boat building and repairing, motor vehicle equipment, trailer coaches, recreation vehicles, and railroad equipment are among the more important employers in this sector. Dominant is the Boeing Corporation, with its aircraft operations in Washington. Recent years have seen an increase in smaller firms producing trailers, campers, and other recreational vehicles and equipment.

In the Pacific Northwest SIC 28, "chemicals and allied products," includes establishments manufacturing and processing fertilizers, industrial chemicals, soaps and detergents, and paints and varnishes. East of the Cascades agricultural chemicals are relatively important in such areas as Yakima County, the Tri-Cities areas, Lewiston, and southeastern Idaho. These locations reflect both agricultural markets and the presence of phosphate deposits in southern Idaho. The broader mix of chemicals produced west of the Cascades is a consequence of a larger, more varied market. Numerous chemicals are produced for industrial consumers, such as wood products firms.

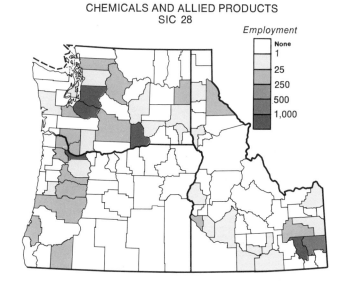

CHEMICALS AND ALLIED PRODUCTS
SIC 28

Employment
None
1
25
250
500
1,000

SHOPPING CENTERS. ▲ Columbia Center, Kennewick, Washington

▼ Lloyd Center and Portland business district Willamette River and Portland harbor

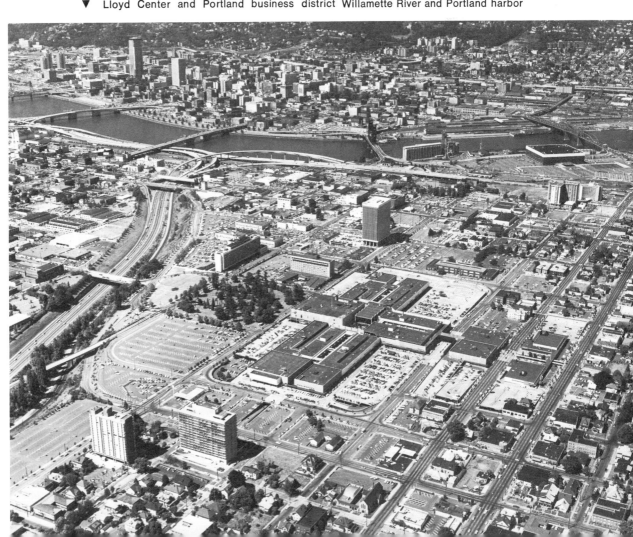

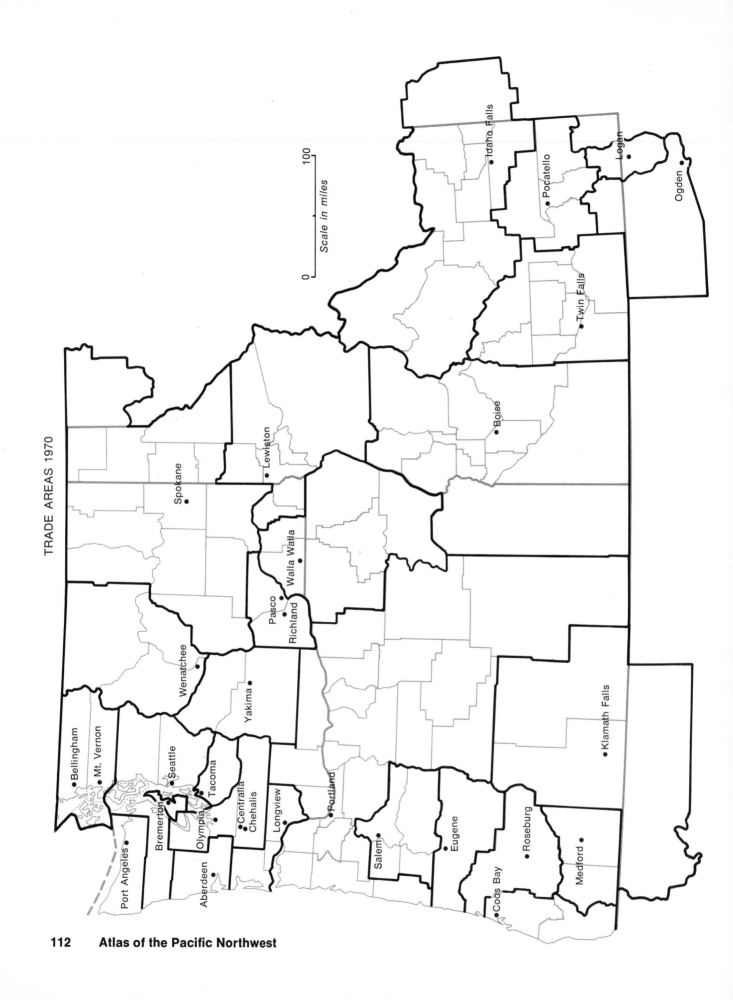

TRADE AREAS 1970

Scale in miles

100

0

Idaho Falls

Pocatello

Logan

Ogden

Twin Falls

Boise

Lewiston

Spokane

Walla Walla

Pasco

Richland

Wenatchee

Yakima

Klamath Falls

Bellingham

Mt. Vernon

Seattle

Tacoma

Olympia

Centralia

Chehalis

Longview

Portland

Salem

Eugene

Roseburg

Medford

Coos Bay

Bremerton

Aberdeen

Port Angeles

Trade and Services ———————————————————————— Ray M. Northam

WHILE EVERY URBAN CENTER performs the functions of offering goods and services to some degree, some may have particular emphasis on one or more specific activities in the tertiary sector. Therefore, various levels or degrees of employment in a particular tertiary function are considered in this section to identify discrete characteristics of individual trade and service centers. For this purpose, different levels of employment in a given trade or service activity are identified by use of standard deviations.

Standard deviations have to do with the variation from an average, which in this case is the average percent of the urban labor force contributed by a given activity, considering all urban centers in the Pacific Northwest. One standard deviation above the mean or average includes 34% of the cases and one standard deviation below the mean includes the same proportion of cases below the average. Two standard deviations include approximately 48% of the cases above and below the mean.

Using this procedure, it is possible to identify those trade and service centers that are slightly or significantly above and below the mean. For example, a given urban center may have a slight emphasis in financial services (within one standard deviation above the mean), while another may have a major deficiency in provision of the same service (within two standard deviations below the mean). This explanatory statement is essential to interpretation of the maps in this section. The maps showing degrees of variation from the average of all cities in the Pacific Northwest indicate the degrees of emphasis or deficiency in a particular trade or service activity, not the amount of employment in that activity. A given city may have hundreds of people engaged in a particular activity, yet this number (as a proportion of the labor force of that city) may represent a deficiency in relation to the average percent of the work force in this activity in all cities of the region.

It can be noted from the maps in this section that a given city may have strengths or deficiencies in a number of trade and service activities or may have strengths or deficiencies in none; i.e., it may have average or near average employment in all activities.

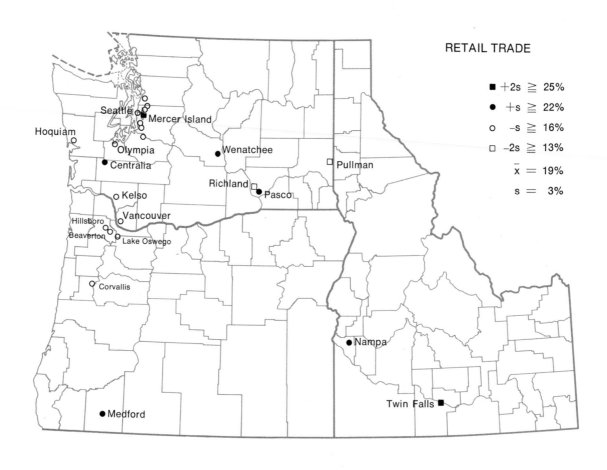

RETAIL TRADE

■ +2s ≧ 25%
● +s ≧ 22%
○ −s ≧ 16%
□ −2s ≧ 13%
x̄ = 19%
s = 3%

Seattle
Mercer Island
Hoquiam
Olympia
Centralia
Wenatchee
Pullman
Kelso
Richland
Pasco
Vancouver
Hillsboro
Beaverton
Lake Oswego
Corvallis
Nampa
Twin Falls
Medford

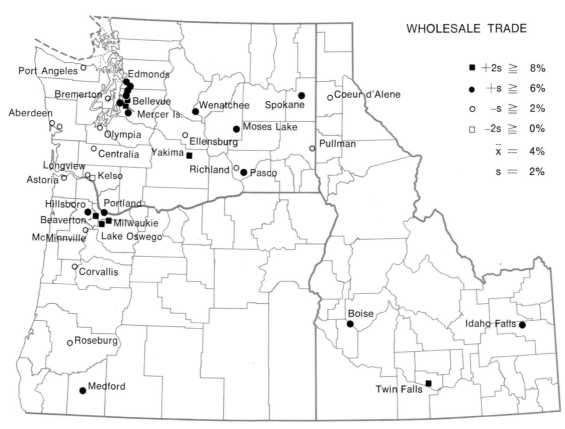

WHOLESALE TRADE

■ +2s ≧ 8%
● +s ≧ 6%
○ −s ≧ 2%
□ −2s ≧ 0%
x̄ = 4%
s = 2%

Port Angeles
Edmonds
Bremerton
Bellevue
Aberdeen
Mercer Is.
Wenatchee
Spokane
Coeur d'Alene
Olympia
Moses Lake
Centralia
Ellensburg
Yakima
Pullman
Longview
Richland
Pasco
Kelso
Astoria
Hillsboro
Portland
Beaverton
Milwaukie
McMinnville
Lake Oswego
Corvallis
Boise
Idaho Falls
Roseburg
Medford
Twin Falls

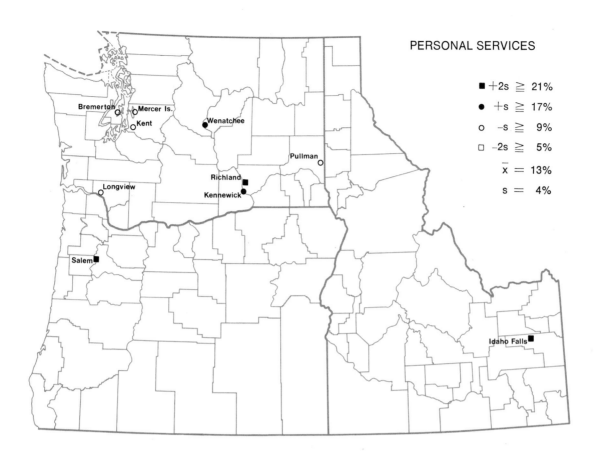

PERSONAL SERVICES

■ +2s ≧ 21%
● +s ≧ 17%
○ −s ≧ 9%
□ −2s ≧ 5%
x̄ = 13%
s = 4%

Bremerton
Mercer Is.
Kent
Wenatchee
Pullman
Richland
Longview
Kennewick
Salem
Idaho Falls

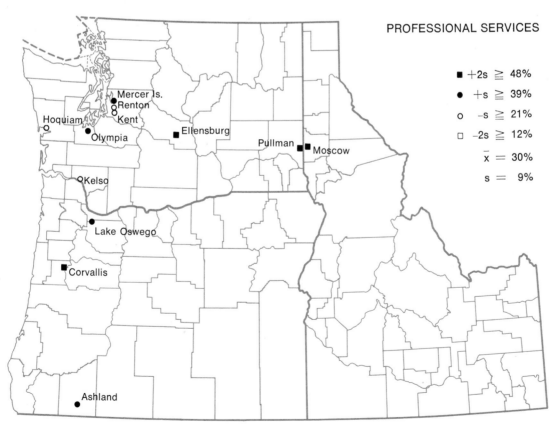

PROFESSIONAL SERVICES

■ +2s ≧ 48%
● +s ≧ 39%
○ −s ≧ 21%
□ −2s ≧ 12%
x̄ = 30%
s = 9%

Mercer Is.
Renton
Hoquiam
Kent
Olympia
Ellensburg
Pullman
Moscow
Kelso
Lake Oswego
Corvallis
Ashland

Trade and Services   115

Recreation ———————————————————— Oliver H. Heintzelman

THE PACIFIC NORTHWEST is endowed with a wealth of resources for a varied and satisfying use of leisure time. There seems to be no limit to active participation in all types of sport. A harmonious combination of spectacular scenery, natural wonders, man-developed landscapes, and economic activities enchant the vacationist and sightseer. Thousands of acres have been reserved for recreation. Millions of dollars have been spent on development. Parks and play areas are accessible through a network of highways. Miles of forest and mountain trails tap primitive and wilderness reserves. Recreation with all its intricate ramifications and tourism hold a firm position as a wealth producer and continually press other activities for economic supremacy and land use in the region.

Mountains are one of the great scenic and recreation assets; they either dominate or constitute the background for every landscape. Northern Idaho is characterized by rugged topography of the Rockies and associated ranges. The Olympics and Willapa Hills parallel the Washington coast. Spurs of the forest-covered Coast Range of Oregon form one of the most picturesque shorelines of America. Oregon and Washington are divided into two distinct regions by the peak-studded Cascade wall. The Klamath Mountains cover southwestern Oregon, the Blue and Wallowa cluster occupies the northeastern corner, and Steens Mountain, cut by spectacular glaciated valleys, is in the southeast.

In sharp contrast to the mountains are the lowlands of the Puget Sound Trough and the Willamette Valley, the broad plains of the Snake, interior valleys, sea-facing lowlands, and the high, dry desert plateaus east of the Cascades. Natural wonders include features of erosion, glaciation, and vulcanism illustrated by gorges and canyons of the Columbia and Snake rivers, Dry Falls, lava flows, cinder buttes, and majestic Crater Lake.

Water shares an equal recreation role. The Pacific Ocean, with a coastline of sandy beaches, coves, and rugged headlands, outlines the western boundary of the Pacific Northwest. Western Washington is penetrated by the sheltered waters of island-dotted Puget Sound. A wealth of lakes ranges from forest-rimmed alpine ponds to larger bodies such as Chelan, Coeur d'Alene, and Klamath. Anglers are attracted by the coast and by snow-fed mountain streams and numerous rivers famed for game fish.

Characterizing the Pacific Northwest are magnificent green stands of conifers. Hardwoods add variety with their seasonal colors. Flowering shrubs brighten forest landscapes and a profusion of wild flowers spice the spring and summer season. Vegetation zones extend from temperate rain forests and colorful mountain meadows to grey-green desert sage.

The natural scene is enriched by an abundance of wildlife. Herds of deer, elk, and antelope graze in forest reserves, parks, and on rangeland. Upland game birds are plentiful and flocks of waterfowl populate inland and coastal waters.

Past and present activities of man contribute to nature's bounty and furnish interesting and stimulating recreation outlets. The historical background is associated with memories of explorations, battles, pioneer treks, gold rushes, and other reminders of lusty settlement and expansion. Bridges and dams for power and irrigation represent skillful engineering feats. Basic economies draw visitors to logging and milling operations, mining and commercial fishing activities, and industrial plants. Contrasts in agriculture are depicted by seas of wheat, orchards, brilliant fields of flowering bulbs, irrigated crops, beef cattle, sheep, and dairying. The charm of the rural scene is enhanced by towns in various stages of growth. Urban life is exemplified by Portland, Spokane, Boise, and Puget Sound cities.

The Pacific Northwest—treasure chest of recreation for man's discovery and enjoyment, land of infinite landscapes delighting the eye and enhancing the spirit of the outdoors.

TOURISTS

(in millions)

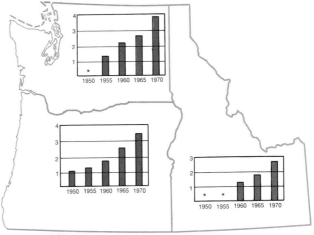

Tourist Expenditures

in 100 millions of dollars

* No Data Available

*no data available

Federal Agencies

The federal government controls and administers the major portion of the outdoor recreational raw material of the Pacific Northwest. The National Park system is dedicated to the preservation and recreational use of four spectacular parks within the area. The National Forest Service, under multiple-use management, offers opportunities for a gamut of recreation activities and aesthetic experiences. The Service has constructed numerous forest camps and thousands of miles of trails. The paramount trail of the West, the Washington-Oregon section of the Pacific Crest Trail, is within the region and provides access to majestic natural landscapes where man is ephemeral. The Bureau of Sport Fisheries and the Wildlife Service perform valuable recreation functions. The Bureau of Land Management devotes a portion of its effort to recreation and indirectly the Bureau of Reclamation and the Corps of Engineers are contributors.

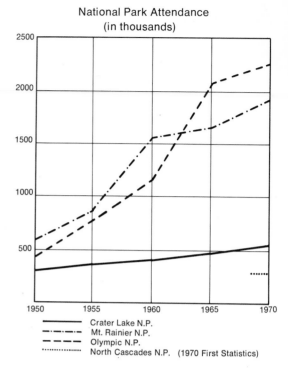

National Park Attendance
(in thousands)

Crater Lake N.P.
Mt. Rainier N.P.
Olympic N.P.
North Cascades N.P.   (1970 First Statistics)

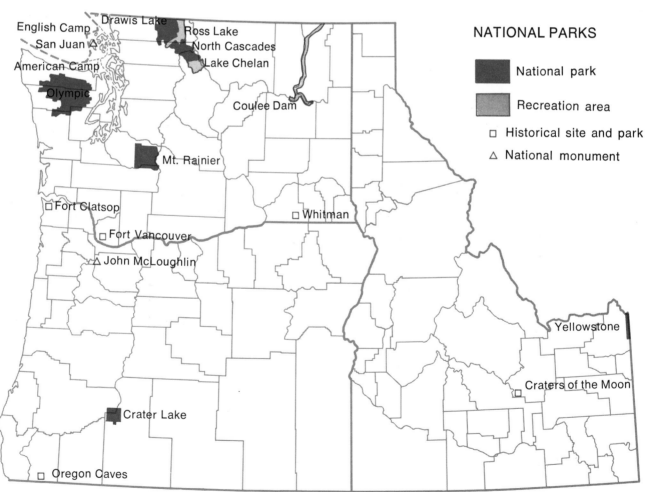

NATIONAL PARKS

■ National park

▨ Recreation area

□ Historical site and park

△ National monument

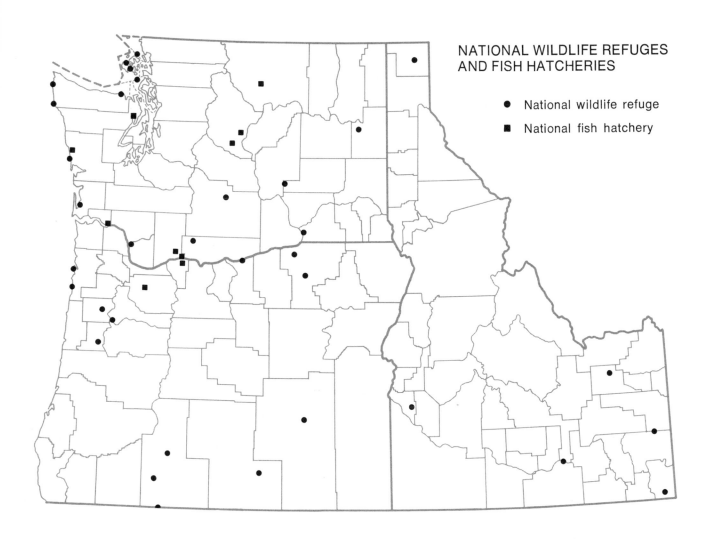

NATIONAL WILDLIFE REFUGES
AND FISH HATCHERIES

● National wildlife refuge

■ National fish hatchery

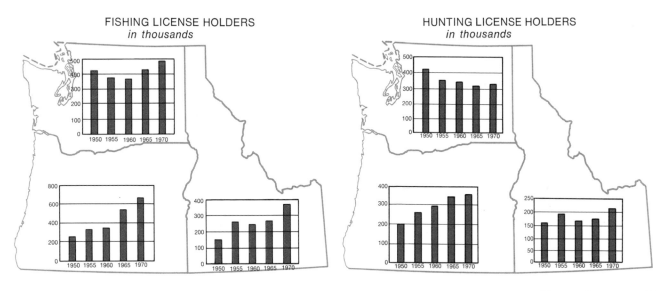

FISHING LICENSE HOLDERS
in thousands

HUNTING LICENSE HOLDERS
in thousands

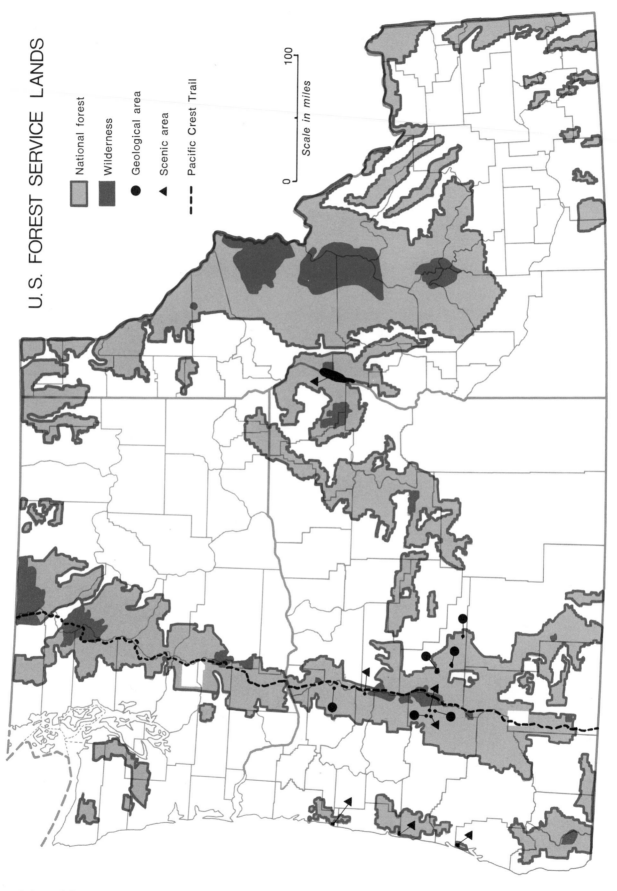

U.S. FOREST SERVICE LANDS

National forest
Wilderness
● Geological area
▲ Scenic area
-- Pacific Crest Trail

Scale in miles

0   100

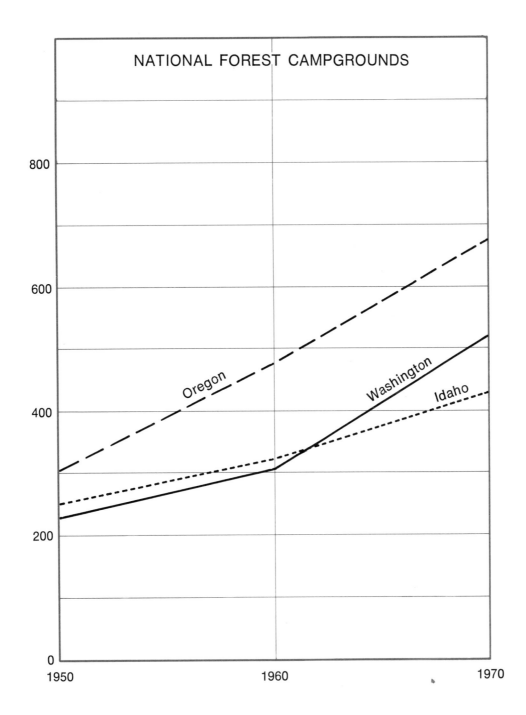

NATIONAL FOREST CAMPGROUNDS

Oregon

Washington

Idaho

Campgrounds in National Forests

	1950	1960	1970
Oregon	303	475	676
Washington	231	309	521
Idaho	253	324	431

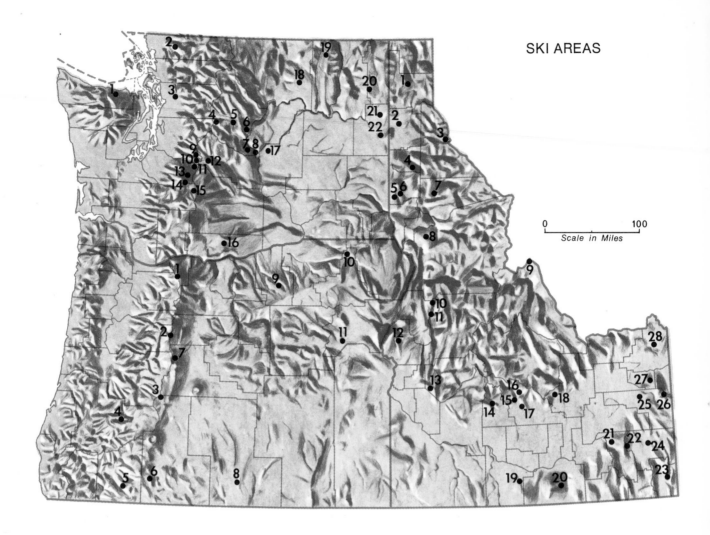

SKI AREAS

0   100
Scale in Miles

Key To Ski Areas Map

Oregon

1. Mount Hood
     Timberline
     Mount Hood Meadows
     Multorpor
     Red Devil
     Cooper Spur
     Snowbunny Lodge
     Summit
2. Hoodoo Ski Bowl
3. Willamette Pass
4. Taft Mountain
5. Mount Ashland
6. Tomahawk
7. Mount Bachelor
9. Arbuckle Mountain
10. Spout Springs
11. Anthony Lakes

Washington

1. Hurricane Ridge
2. Mount Baker
3. Mount Pilchuck
4. Sno County—Stevens Pass
5. Yodelin
6. Leavenworth
7. Mission Ridge
8. Squilchuck
9. Alpental
10. Snoqualmie
11. Ski Acres
12. Syak
13. Crystal Mountain
14. Paradise
15. White Pass Village
16. Satus Pass
17. Badger Mountain
18. Loup Loup
19. Sitzmark
20. Chewelah Mountain
21. Mount Spokane
22. Holiday Hills

Idaho

1. Schweitzer Basin
2. Flying H Dude Ranch
3. Lookout Pass
4. North South Bowl
5. Moscow-Mountain Acres
6. Moscow Mountain
7. Bald Mountain
8. Snowhaven
9. Lost Trail
10. Brundage
11. Payette Lakes
12. Hitt
13. Bogus Basin
14. Soldier Mountain
15. Sun Valley
16. Kinderhorn
17. Rotorun
18. Blizzard Mountain
19. Magic Mountain
20. Pomerelle
21. Caribou
22. Skyline
23. Montpelier
24. Soda Springs
25. Taylor Mountain
26. Pine Basin
27. Kelly Canyon
28. Bear Gulch

Information Sources: Outdoor Recreation

STATE

Idaho

Idaho Bureau of Mines and Geology
University of Idaho
Moscow, Idaho 83843

Idaho Fish and Game Department
P. O. Box 25
Boise, Idaho 83701

Idaho Historical Society
610 N. Julia Davis Drive
Boise, Idaho 83701

Idaho State Dept. of
  Commerce and Development
Room 108 Statehouse
Boise, Idaho 83701

State of Idaho—Dept. of Highways
P. O. Box 7129
Boise, Idaho 83707

Oregon

Fish Commission of Oregon
307 State Office Building
Salem, Oregon 97310

Oregon State Game Commission
P. O. Box 3503
Portland, Oregon 97208

Oregon State Dept. of Forestry
2600 State Street
Salem, Oregon 97310

Oregon State Dept. of Transportation
Parks and Recreation Division
State Highway Building
Salem, Oregon 97310

Oregon State Dept. of Transportation
State Highway Division
Travel Information Section
State Highway Building
Salem, Oregon 97310

Washington

Public Information Office
Washington State Parks and
  Recreation Commission
P. O. Box 1128
Olympia, Washington 98501

Tourist Promotion Division
Washington State Department of
  Commerce and Economic Development
General Administration Building
Olympia, Washington 98501

Tourist Division
Washington State Dept. of
  Natural Resources
Public Lands Building
Olympia, Washington 98501

Washington State Dept. of Fisheries
115 General Administration Building
Olympia, Washington 98501

Washington State Dept. of Game
600 North Capital Way
Olympia, Washington 98501

FEDERAL

Bureau of Land Management

Idaho State Office
P. O. Box 2237
Boise, Idaho 83701

Oregon State Office
P. O. Box 2965
Portland, Oregon 97208

Spokane District (Washington Office)
West 920 Riverside Avenue
Spokane, Washington 99201

Bureau of Outdoor Recreation

Regional Director
407 U. S. Court House
Seattle, Washington 98104

Bureau of Reclamation

Regional Director
P. O. Box 8008
Boise, Idaho 83707

Bureau of Sport Fisheries and Wildlife

Regional Director
1365 N. Orchard Street
Boise, Idaho 83704

Regional Director
P. O. Box 3737
Portland, Oregon 97208

Corps of Engineers

District Engineer
P. O. Box 2946
Portland, Oregon 97208

District Engineer
Bldg. 619, City-County Airport
Walla Walla, Washington 99362

National Park Service

District Director
Room 1051
Federal Office Building
Seattle, Washington 98104

U. S. Forest Service

Regional Forester
Federal Building
Missoula, Montana 59801

Regional Forester
Federal Office Building
324-25th Street
Ogden, Utah 84401

Regional Forester
P. O. Box 3623
Portland, Oregon 97208

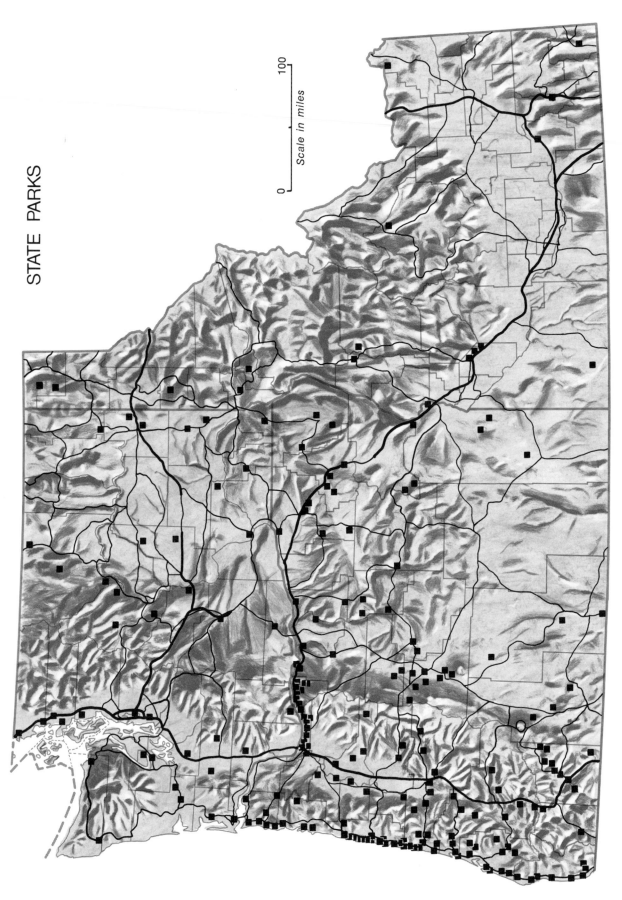

STATE PARKS

Scale in miles

0   100

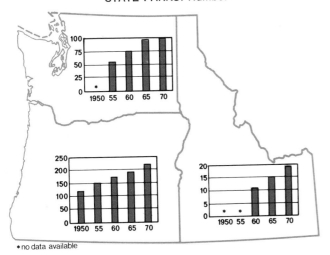

STATE PARKS: Number

*no data available

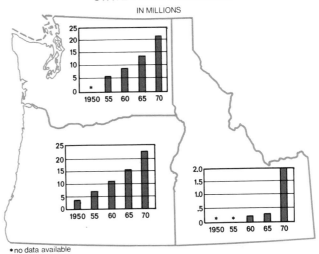

STATE PARKS: Attendance
IN MILLIONS

*no data available

BICYCLE PATHS IN OREGON

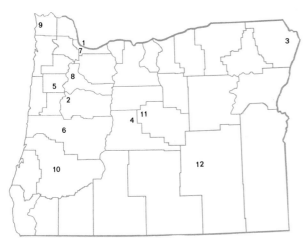

KEY TO MAP

		Miles
1.	Mount Hood Highway	5.1
2.	Albany-Junction City Highway	2.8
3.	Joseph-Wallowa Lake Highway	.9
4.	McKenzie Highway	3.0
5.	Monmouth-Independence Highway	1.5
6.	Junction City-Eugene Highway	5.5
7.	Oswego Highway	2.5
8.	Pacific Highway East	1.3
9.	Oregon Coast Highway	3.3
10.	Coos Bay-Roseburg Highway	1.2
11.	Madras-Prineville Highway	1.5
12.	Central Oregon Highway	2.3

LONG-RANGE PLANS

(1) *Coast Route*—A scenic coastal bike route is envisioned from the California border to Astoria.

(2) *Columbia River Route*—A scenic route from Astoria along the Columbia River to the Multnomah Falls recreational area and to provide intra-town connections.

(3) *Portland to Eugene Route*—A continuous route through the Willamette Valley. Routes to focus on points of interest such as Champoeg Park, Silver Creek Falls, and the Willamette River.

(4) *Willamette Valley to Coast Routes*—To provide access from the population centers in the valley to the coast in conjunction with additional intra-town connections.

(5) *Grants Pass, Medford, and Klamath Falls*—Scenic loop routes to provide a system incorporating recreational facilities and points of interest along with the intra-town routes.

(6) *Eastern Oregon Routes*—Scenic loops and a system incorporating recreational facilities.

LAPIDARY MATERIAL SITES

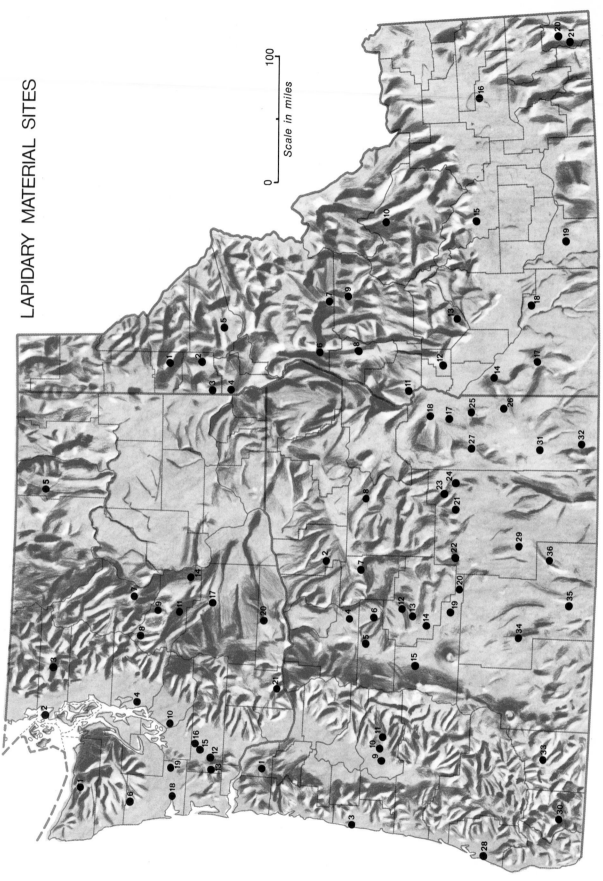

Scale in miles

0   100

Key to Lapidary Map

OREGON

1. Vernonia, Columbia County—agate and jasper (Nehalem River gravels)
2. Hardman, Morrow County—agate and opal (fire) in thundereggs (White Ranch and Opal Butte)
3. "Oregon Beaches" (Wecoma Beach to Florence)—agate, jasper, and sagenite
4. Antelope, Wasco County—agate (moss) and jasper (famous old locality)
5. Willowdale, Jefferson County—thundereggs (Priday Ranch, Kennedy Ranch, and Friends Ranch)
6. Ashwood, Jefferson County — agate, petrified wood, and thundereggs (one of the richest deposits in the state)
7. Spray, Wheeler County—jasper and agate (Corncob Ranch)
8. Middle Fork of John Day River—agate and petrified wood (China Diggin's, Sunshine Flat, Lick Creek, Windy Point, and Howard Meadows)
9. Calapooya River, Linn County—sagenite, amethyst-agate, and petrified wood
10. Lebanon, Linn County—carnelian and agate (2 miles south), petrified wood (10 miles north)
11. Sweet Home, Linn County—petrified wood and agate (3 miles southwest)
12. Ochoco Mountain, Crook County—thundereggs, agate, and jasper
13. Crook River, Crook County—plume agate (Carey Ranch and Eagle Rock)
14. Bear Creek, Crook County—agate (moss) and jasper
15. Peterson's Rock Garden, Deschutes County—large rock exhibit
16. South Fork Crook River, Crook County—agate
17. Harper, Malheur County—thundereggs and petrified wood (20-30 miles south)
18. Jamison, Malheur County—bog agates and petrified wood (8 miles northeast)
19. Hampton Butte, Deschutes County—agate, jasper, and petrified wood
20. Glass Butte, Deschutes County—red and black obsidian (near Hampton)
21. Buchanan Lane, Harney County—agate, jasper, and petrified wood
22. Burns, Harney County—large obsidian flow (7 miles west)
23. Riverside, Harney County—agate, jasper, and petrified wood
24. Stinkingwater Mountain, Harney County—agate and petrified wood (north and south of Highway 20)
25. Succor Creek, Malheur County—thundereggs and jasper (Graveyard Point Area)
26. Jordan Valley, Malheur County—petrified wood
27. Dry Creek, Malheur County—petrified wood and agate
28. "Southern Oregon Beaches" (Bandon to Gold Beach)—petrified wood
29. Harney Lake, Harney County—petrified wood and oolite (2 miles south)
30. Kerby, Josephine County—oregonite and grossulanite garnet
31. Rome, Malheur County—"snakeskin agate" (15 miles southwest)
32. McDermitt, Malheur County—petrified wood (15 miles west)
33. Camp White-Eagle Point, Jackson County—agate (dendrites) and sagenite
34. Paisley, Lake County—agate (Chewancan River)
35. Lakeview, Lake County — thundereggs (Dry Creek) and petrified wood (Quartz Mountain)
36. Plush, Lake County—feldspar (Rabbit Creek) and jasper, agate, and opal (fire) (Hart Mountain)

WASHINGTON

1. Crescent Bay, Clallam County—jasper ("North Coast" beaches)
2. Anacortes, San Juan Islands—jasper
3. Concrete, Skagit County—jade (23.8 miles east)
4. Issaquah, King County—amber (7 miles southeast)
5. Republic, Ferry County—garnet and agate (15 miles east)
6. Salmon River, Grays Harbor County—agate
7. Cashmere, Chelan County—rose quartz
8. Lake Cle Elum, Kittitas County—geodes and quartz crystals
9. Thorp, Kittitas County—crystal geodes (near Frost Mountain)
10. Nisqually, Pierce County—petrified wood
11. Ellensburg, Kittitas County—agate (Jack Creek) and petrified wood (Saddle to Kittitas—one of the world's most extensive deposits)
12. Toledo, Lewis County—jasper and bloodstone (25 miles northeast)
13. Adna, Lewis County—petrified wood, carnelian, jasper
14. Beverly, Kittitas County—petrified wood (5 miles south)
15. Chehalis, Lewis County — carnelian, petrified wood (many locations)
16. Tono, Lewis County—agate (many locations)
17. Yakima, Yakima County—petrified wood (firing range)
18. Aberdeen, Grays Harbor County—jasper
19. Porter, Grays Harbor County—fossil crab (just south of town)
20. Sunnyside-Bickleton-Roosevelt — petrified wood, agate, and jasper
21. Stevenson, Skamania County—jasper, various bloodstone (Wind River)

IDAHO

1. Fernwood, Benewah County—garnet (star, in schist on Emerald Creek)
2. Bovill, Latah County—garnet (star, in placer)
3. Moscow, Latah County—garnet (in schist)
4. Lewiston, Nez Perce County—opal (fire) (in rims 6 miles west)
5. Pierce, Clearwater County—garnet (Rhodes and Oro Fino creeks)
6. Riggins, Idaho County—jasper and agate (John Day Creek, 12 miles north), garnet (in Salmon River placers)
7. Warren, Idaho County—topaz and quartz crystals (Paddy Creek)
8. New Meadows, Adams County—rhodonite (near Tamarack, 6 miles south), sapphire (near Rock Flat)
9. Yellow Pine, Valley County—agate (cinnibar)
10. Challis, Custer County—jasper and agate (in low hills, radius 10 miles)
11. Weiser, Washington County — agate (on Hog Creek, 10-15 miles northwest)
12. Emmet, Gem County—opal (fire), agate, jasper, and petrified wood (Pearl and Willow creeks)
13. Idaho City, Boise County—opal (Moore Creek)
14. Marshing, Owyhee County—opal (fire) (Givern Springs, 15 miles south), jasper and queenstone (10 miles south on US 95)
15. Bellevue, Blaine County—agate (dendritic and moss) and sagenite (Muldoon Summit and Little Wood River Res.)
16. Firth, Bingham County—black *tempsiki* (approximately 20 miles south)
17. Silver City, Owyhee County—agate and corundum
18. Bruneau, Owyhee County—amethyst, agate, and jasper
19. Rogerson, Twin Falls County—thundereggs and agate (dendritic) and sagenite
20. Montpelier, Bear Lake County—jasper
21. Paris, Bear Lake County—jasper